LINCOLN CHRISTIAN COLLEGE AN

P9-DES-427

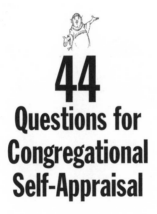

44
Questions for
Congregational
Self-Appraisal

LINCOLN CHRISTIAN COLLEGE AND SEMINARY

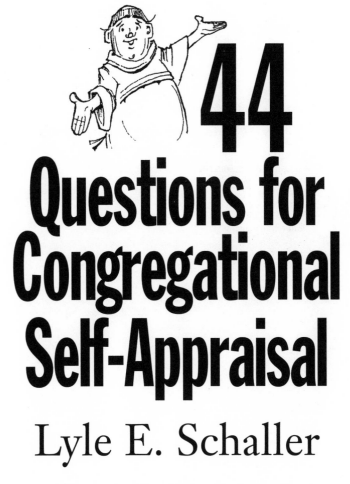

44 Questions for Congregational Self-Appraisal

Lyle E. Schaller

Illustrated by Edward Lee Tucker

Abingdon Press
Nashville

44 QUESTIONS FOR CONGREGATIONAL SELF-APPRAISAL

Copyright © 1998 by Abingdon Press

All rights reserved.
No part of this work may be reproduced or transmitted in any form or by any means, electronic or mechanical, including photocopying and recording, or by any information storage or retrieval system, except as may be expressly permitted by the 1976 Copyright Act or in writing from the publisher. Requests for permission should be addressed to Abingdon Press, 201 Eighth Avenue South, P.O. Box 801, Nashville TN 37202-0801.

This book is printed on recycled, acid-free elemental-chlorine-free paper.

Library of Congress Cataloging-in-Publication Data

Schaller, Lyle E.
    44 questions for congregational self-appraisal / Lyle E. Schaller ; illustrated by Edward Lee Tucker.
       p. c m.
    Includes bibliographical references.
    ISBN 0-687-08840-2 (pbk. : alk. paper)
    1. Church management.   I. Title.
BV652.S276   1998
254—dc21   97-42718
                                              CIP

Scripture quotations unless otherwise labeled are from the New Revised Standard Version Bible, Copyright © 1989 by the Division of Christian Education of the National Council of the Churches of Christ in the USA. Used by permission.

98 99 00 01 02 03 04 05 06 07—10 9 8 7 6 5 4 3 2 1

MANUFACTURED IN THE UNITED STATES OF AMERICA

To Nancy and
The Contemporary Choir

93371

CONTENTS

INTRODUCTION. 11

CHAPTER ONE: Where Do We Begin? 21

Two Responses 22
Which Planning Model?. 23
    A. What Are the Expectations We Project?. 25
    B. Who Is Our Number One Constituency? 30
    C. What Is Our Niche? 34
    D. How Large Is Our Parish? 38
    E. What Is Our Approach to Ministry? 39
    F. What Do We Do Best? 43
    G. What Is Our Driving Motivation?. 44
    H. What Do We Expect of Our Pastor and Staff? 48

CHAPTER TWO: What Do the Numbers Tell Us? 58

    A. How Large Is This Congregation? 59
    B. What Is the Ratio? 64
    C. What Is the Median Tenure? 65
    D. What Is the Frequency of Worship Attendance? 67
    E. What Is the Turnover Rate?. 75
    F. What Are the Sources of Our New Members? 78
    G. How Many Baptisms? 80
    H. Where Do Our People Live? 81
    I. What Is the Age Distribution of Our Members? 82

J. What Is the Marital and Family Distribution?........ 84

K. When Was This Congregation Founded?............ 87

CHAPTER THREE: What Is Our Purpose? What Is Our Community Image?......................... 89

A. What Is the Operational Statement of Purpose?....... 89

B. Are We Happy with That Operational Statement?..... 92

C. How Do Others See Us? 93

D. Are You Happy with That Image? 96

CHAPTER FOUR: Who Will Be Tomorrow's New Members?.................................. 98

A. How Long Is the List of Prospective Future Members? .. 99

B. Who Is Responsible for That List? 99

C. How Many First-Time Visitors Worship with Us Each Weekend?............................. 99

D. How Many New Face-to-Face Groups?............ 100

E. How Many New Full Members Did We Receive Last Year?................................. 101

F. Has That Ratio of New Members Received to Resident Full Members Been Going Up or Down During the Past Several Years?........................... 101

G. What Are the Ages and Marital Characteristics of Our New Members? 102

H. Can We Interview Our Past Visitors?............. 102

CHAPTER FIVE: How Are We Organized? 107

A. Permission-Giving or Permission-Withholding?...... 107

B. Abundance or Scarcity? 108

C. Care of Members or Welcome to Strangers?........ 110

D. What Is the Crucial Dividing Line Between the Laity and the Paid Staff? 111

E. What Is Our Self-Image? 112

F. What Is the Stance of Our Pastor?................ 113

CHAPTER SIX: Means-to-an-End Questions........ *116*

    A. How Much Land Do We Need? *118*
    B. How Much Money Do We Need? *119*
    C. How Much Staff Do We Need? *127*
    D. What Are the Criteria and Trends for Designing
      Our Schedule? *131*

CHAPTER SEVEN: How Large Should We Build It? .. *141*

    Twenty-one Questions............................ *142*
    What Else? *156*

CHAPTER EIGHT: Three Fork-in-the-Road Questions *158*

    A. Teaching or Learning? *159*
    B. Youth or Families? *166*
    C. How Many in a Group? *172*

NOTES *178*

Who would be interested in reading a book on congregational self-appraisal?

To answer that question, we need to divide the 350,000 to 400,000 Christian congregations in North America into three groups. The largest group, perhaps three-quarters of the total, displays varying degrees of interest in planning for a new era in their history. In many of them, however, a number of today's leaders are convinced that the time has come to become more intentional in their ministry. Most of the planning models from which they can choose require a realistic self-appraisal. What is contemporary reality? What is our current beginning point or

Are we ready to choose a realistic model of self-appraisal?
—FRIAR TUCK

baseline from which we project our plans for ministry into the third millennium?

That group of churches constitutes the primary constituency for this book. Their leaders recognize the value of a realistic self-appraisal as an early step in their planning process. The questions in this book are designed to stimulate, expand, and challenge their thinking.

Another 15 to 20 percent of the churches, perhaps more, organize their self-evaluation process around seven questions. Frequently this is a highly informal effort and is not part of a larger design to become more intentional in ministry. What are the seven questions?

1. Do we have enough money to pay all our bills? Have our total receipts been increasing or decreasing?
2. What is the condition of our real estate?
3. Is our membership going up or down?
4. How is the Sunday school doing?
5. Is worship attendance up or down?
6. Are our people reasonably happy with how things are going here now? If they are unhappy, what can be done about that?
7. How many dollars are we sending away for others to do missions on our behalf? Is that total up or down?

Frequently the trustees and other officers both raise and answer these questions. At least one or two usually are addressed to the pastor for a response. This book has been written to expand the number and variety of questions to be asked in the self-appraisal process in these congregations.

The remaining 5 to 10 percent of all congregations are at the other end of the ecclesiastical spectrum. They frequently ask only five or six questions in their self-appraisal efforts. Many of the congregations in this third group fit into the category described in chapter 1 as Kingdom-building churches. Their top priority is to faithfully respond to the call to build God's kingdom. A far lower priority is given to enhancing the institutional strength of that particular congregation. Their self-appraisal questions focus on transforming the lives of people, not on institutional concerns. Evangelism and missions, rather than real estate and money, drive the decisions that allocate scarce resources. Those are the threads running through the short list of questions that are at the top of their self-appraisal effort.

1. How many lives are being transformed through our ministries? Is that number increasing or decreasing?
2. How effective are we in challenging, enlisting, training, placing, and supporting our people as volunteers in off-campus ministries?
3. What is the new outreach ministry the Great Commission is calling us to pioneer? How do we reach and serve the people that the churches in this community currently are not reaching? How can we help other congregations learn from what we discover as we pioneer new ministries in obedience to the Great Commission?
4. What are we doing to support the work of others in fulfilling the Great Commission in other parts of the world?
5. As the years roll by, is God challenging us to identify and accept a new role as a Kingdom-building church?

6. (Maybe) What changes do we need to make to enable us to reach and serve a broader slice of the total population living around us?

While many of the leaders in this third group of churches may see this as an excessively institution-centered volume, it is hoped that they will find several of these questions useful additions to their self-appraisal efforts.

The first chapter of this book lifts up eight questions that many congregational leaders will find useful as they seek to describe contemporary reality in their congregation. The first question is a crucial fork-in-the-road question that is one of the most meaningful ways to distinguish one congregation from another. Is this a high-expectation congregation or a low-expectation congregation? The seventh question raises a parallel issue. Is this *primarily* a Kingdom-building congregation or *primarily* a congregation-building church? For many leaders the answer to that question will determine which will be the relevant questions for the self-appraisal process.

The second chapter raises eleven traditional questions that can be found in most self-study manuals. The two distinctive contributions of this chapter are (a) a larger context for interpreting the data gathered in response to these questions and (b) suggestions on alternative responses to issues illuminated by this data-gathering process.

In choosing which will be the most useful of these questions, it should be noted that frequently what is measured or counted is what becomes a high priority. Counting the dollars sent away for benevolences may not result in a high quality ministry with families that include teenagers. Too often congregational leaders count and report what is a relatively low priority in their ministry plan.

The third chapter shifts the focus to the more basic question of purpose. The traditional approach to this issue is to begin with a blank sheet of paper and formulate what *should* be the central reason for the existence of this congregation. That is an appropriate beginning point for those responsible for plant-ing a new mission. The central theme of this chapter, however, is the need to define contemporary reality. In realistic terms what is the current operational statement of purpose? Four questions are suggested as the way to respond to that issue.

Every Christian congregation can be described as a passing parade of people. Every year newcomers join that parade while others leave. The fourth chapter raises eight questions designed to help leaders evaluate their efforts to reach newcomers to the community as well as the unchurched population. Potentially the most valuable information to be gained from this part of the self-appraisal process will come from first-time visitors who never returned or, perhaps, returned a second time before continuing their search for a new church home.

'THO YOU MAY NEVER COME BACK, COULD YOU GIVE US SOME FEEDBACK?

Those who come only once or twice can help us in our self-appraisal?

—FRIAR TUCK.

Chapter 5 raises six questions that will help you determine whether your congregation is organized to make preserving the status quo the top priority or to welcome creativity, innovation, change, and a new tomorrow that will be filled with surprises.

The biggest threat to effective congregational planning for a new tomorrow is that means-to-an-end question that will float to the top of the agenda. Many leaders are more comfortable studying issues such as real estate, staffing, money, and schedules than they are reflecting on more intangible and subjective questions such as identity, purpose, role, and God's call. In an effort to keep these means-to-an-end questions from dominating the self-appraisal process, four means-to-an-end questions are reviewed in the sixth chapter, not the first. A better reason for placing them in the sixth chapter is they can be discussed more intelligently if they are not even raised until the fundamental questions on identity, purpose, role, and call have been resolved.

One of the consequences of the emergence of an unprecedented number of very large Protestant congregations in North America is the call for constructing new houses of worship. This frequently evokes two questions. When will we be able to construct a new worship center? How large should we build it? The second of these questions is the theme of the seventh chapter. The answer is, please be patient and reflect on twenty-one other questions before deciding to construct that new big room for worship. Incidentally, since this question is not on the current agenda of most congregations, we will not count it in fulfilling the promise for *44 Questions for Congregational Self-Appraisal!*

The last chapter raises three questions that reflect radical changes in how we do ministry in North America in the closing years of the second millennium. The most widely discussed is the shift from teaching to learning. The most challenging is in the responses to the generations born after 1969. The most subtle is a different conceptual framework for describing a congregation. Instead of conceptualizing this as a collection of x number of individuals or y number of families or z number of pledging units, a more useful system is to conceptualize it as a collection of groups of individuals. How many people constitute a group? That is the theme of the last of the forty-four questions in this volume.

In addition to these forty-four basic self-appraisal questions, this volume is enriched by several dozen cartoons lifting up the wisdom, insights, and reflections of that lovable elf, Friar Tuck.

Caution!

Anyone who suggests that their congregation undertake a serious self-appraisal effort should be warned of two probable consequences.

The first is summarized in an ancient bit of conventional wisdom. Education is alienating! Many parents who never attended college discovered that when their eighteen-year-old child came home during Christmas vacation from that first year at the state university. Many husbands discovered it when their wives went back to school. The volunteers serving in a congregational self-appraisal task force often find themselves alienated from other leaders who are convinced today is a carbon copy of 1979 or who are offering suggestions based on an obsolete database.

Overlapping that is what is sometimes described as the *self-identified discrepancy*. When a person discovers the gap between perceived reality and true reality, it often leads to proposals for change. One example is the obese person who looks sideways into a full-length mirror. A second is the person who, after filing federal income taxes, exclaims, "Golly, our income last year was higher than I had thought it would be. I guess I need to start keeping better records." A third is the owner who takes the car in for the 60,000 mile checkup. The estimate is triple what was expected, so the owner decides to trade for a new vehicle. Another is the member of the congregational self-appraisal team. After comparing the reality revealed by the responses to a series of questions with what that person believes that congregation could and should be doing in ministry, this person concludes, "If we don't make some changes around here, by the time I die there won't be anyone left to come to my funeral."

Our Niche...

Formula: True ministry is found when our limited resources match the special needs of others!

—FRIAR TUCK

In other words, if you are happy with the status quo and want to avoid challenging people with the need for change, it may be prudent not to begin the self-appraisal process.

Responding to Denial

Why should a dozen or so members embark on the laborious process of responding to three or four dozen congregational self-appraisal questions? One good reason is to combat denial.

The majority of North American Protestant congregations founded before 1970 are in a state of denial. The most widespread example is the refusal to believe that most of the people born after 1955 bring a different set of expectations to church than are carried by those born before 1940. A second is the definition of what is a meaningful worship experience. A third is the focus of the last chapter. The old conceptual frameworks are becoming obsolete. A fourth is the large regional church

OH-OH! 45 inches?

Self-appraisal
is one way
to combat denial!
—FRIAR TUCK.

has become the successor to the neighborhood congregation, especially among growing numbers of (a) recent immigrants, (b) African Americans, and (c) the generations born after 1942. A fifth example is the changing role of the paid staff from doers to trainers.

What is the most effective response to denial? First, rec-

"... denial is never a source of either hope or creativity!"
—FRIAR TUCK

ognize that denial is never a source of creativity or innovation! Second, flood the system with accurate information describing contemporary reality. The congregational self-appraisal process is one way to combat denial.

CHAPTER ONE

Where Do We Begin?

WE CAN'T GET THERE FROM HERE UNLESS WE KNOW WHERE HERE IS?

THE LOST MINE

And we can't get from here unless we know where we want to go!

—FRIAR TUCK

"Two months after I arrived here, I asked our board to appoint a Long-Range Planning Committee," explained the new minister at the 345-member Grace Church.

"Last week the board appointed the seven members to serve on this special committee. We gave them two assignments. The first was to evaluate our present ministry. The second was to design a five-year ministry plan for our church. Last night the person who was asked to chair this committee called me and asked, 'Where do we begin? What is our first step? How do we go about evaluating our present ministry? Should we begin with an evaluation of the staff? Or of the real estate? Or the finances? What do you think would be the best beginning point? What is the first question this committee should address?'"

Two Responses

The first response is do not begin that self-appraisal process by looking at the staff or the real estate or the financial base.

Many congregational leaders are more comfortable in planning for the future if one of these three sets of questions is at the top of the self-appraisal agenda.

1. What changes are we facing in staffing this congregation? Will our current pastor be leaving in the near future? Has the time come to add a second pastor to the staff? What will be our staff requirements five years from now?
2. What do we need to do to this aging building to prepare for tomorrow? Should we remodel it? Does it require major repairs? Should we install central air conditioning? Should we construct an addition to it? Should we purchase the property next door?
3. Should we pay off our current indebtedness before we make any other plans for the future? Or is our first priority to raise the level of member giving to put us on a sound financial base? Should we first concentrate on building up our endowment funds? Should we "test the market" by first running a capital funds campaign?

Those are all means-to-an-end concerns. Beginning with them will turn out to be a diversionary beginning point. More important, it is impossible to make a meaningful evaluation of means-to-an-end issues until *after* agreement has been reached on the end, on the purpose, and on defining

the reasons for the continued existence of this congregation. Thus a better beginning point would be to focus
on purpose, mission, and
ministry.

**Without a plan,
we could end up
where we don't want to be!**
—*FRIAR TUCK,*

Which Planning Model?

That recommendation, how-
ever, raises another question.
What is the planning model
this special committee will
use? One of many alterna-
tives is to begin by articulat-
ing the vision of what that
committee believes the Lord
is calling this congregation to
be and to be doing in the years ahead. In this planning model,
the second step is to define contemporary reality. The next
step is to make a realistic appraisal of the gap between the
vision or dream and reality of today. The fourth step is to
design a strategy that will move this congregation from
"here" (contemporary reality) to "there" (the translation of
that vision into reality).[1]

In this particular situation, however, the board instructed
the committee to use a different planning model. In somewhat simplified form, this also consists of three steps,
(1) define contemporary reality, (2) articulate the vision for a
new tomorrow, and (3) formulate the strategy to get from
here to there.

What is a good beginning point for a congregational self-
appraisal process? A common answer is to confuse this with
a widely used planning model that calls for defining purpose
and role. That is a useful model for designing the distinctive

WHO BROUGHT
A COMPASS?

For churches to go forward
their leaders need a common
point of reference!

—FRIAR TUCK.

role of a new mission. For the long-established congregation, however, the best beginning points are to agree on what this congregation should look like five or ten years down the road and draw up an accurate description of contemporary reality. What is our starting point as we plan for that new tomorrow?

That can be illustrated by looking briefly at two congregations that meet in buildings a block apart. The first was founded in 1907, peaked in size with an average worship attendance of 235 in 1957, and now averages 120 at worship. The median age of the 340 confirmed members is sixty-two years, and 70 percent have been members here for more than twelve years.

A block away is the meeting place of a congregation that was founded in 1921 and averaged 135 at worship in 1957. During the past two decades, what once was a small and stable farming community and retail center has become a bedroom community for people who want to live in a small town setting and draw a paycheck from the nearby new employment centers. The population of this county seat town has grown from 5,300 twenty years ago to 24,000 today. This second congregation has redefined its identity, accepted a new role as an exurban church, enlarged its physical facilities, expanded the schedule from one to four worship experiences every weekend, and now averages 570 at worship. The median age of the last 200 adult new members is thirty-three years. The current confirmed membership includes 436 people age fourteen and over.

That first congregation averages two or three first-time visitors each Sunday morning, most of whom never return. The second averages ten to fifteen first-time visitors every weekend, and the vast majority return at least once or twice.

Obviously, these two congregations do not share the same beginning point when each begins to plan for tomorrow. The first is far more likely to be driven by institutional survival goals than the second.

What is the best beginning point for a self-appraisal process in your church? One answer is to choose the sequence that appears to fit your unique circumstances and the one with which you will be comfortable.

For many churches a useful sequence will be to begin with the questions in these first two chapters. That can be followed by an analysis of purpose and role. The responses to the questions articulated in these three chapters can be a useful context for responding to the remaining questions.

A. What Are the Expectations We Project?

Perhaps the most rarely used, the most revealing, and the most useful as a predictor of the future beginning point is to identify the expectations projected to those who are members or who want to become members.

This can be stated in at least four different ways.

Vision...

STRANGELY, TO GET OUT OF ANY RUT, WE MUST DIG DEEPER!

—FRIAR TUCK

Discovering our unique role for the future can put our problems behind us!

IT'S SUNDAY... DO I FEEL LIKE GOING *to* CHURCH or THE BEACH?

Where commitment is low, there's a perpetual shortage of volunteers!
— FRIAR TUCK

First, does your congregation expect most adults will be present for one period of time on Sunday morning? Or for two periods of time? Or for three or four periods of time? At one end of this spectrum are the churches that offer the "one hour package." This enables the parents to participate in corporate worship while their children are in Sunday school. Typically this requires an investment of sixty-five to eighty minutes from the time the family arrives until they can be on their way again.

At the other end of this spectrum is the schedule that begins with breakfast at seven o'clock on Sunday morning followed by Sunday school at nine-thirty and worship at eleven. This schedule is designed for the person who wants to combine breakfast with a two-hour adult class, teach in the Sunday school, and also participate in worship. In larger congregations, this schedule begins with breakfast, followed by early worship, then Sunday school meeting in midmorning, followed by the second worship service.

The "one-hour package" projects low expectations. The schedule that is designed to enable adults to be in a class, to be in worship, and to teach in Sunday school projects higher expectations.

A second example of projected expectations is reflected by the combination of the seating capacity of the worship center and the schedule. A typical example is the 400-resident member congregation that worships in a room that will seat

200 and averages 150 at the one service on Sunday morning. Two or three worship services are scheduled for Christmas Eve, Easter, and perhaps Mother's Day. The message is clear: Except for those three high holy days, we expect the majority of our members will stay away from worship on the typical Sunday.

A third example of this question of expectations is described as "the threshold for membership." At one end of this spectrum are those congregations that require prospective new members (a) to participate in a thirty-six- or forty-two- or forty-eight-week class before they are eligible to request to become members, (b) to be regular attenders at worship, (c) to be involved as a volunteer in doing ministry, (d) to be a tither, and (e) to be a member of a continuing class or small group or prayer cell. At the other end of this spectrum are the low-threshold congregations that require only a public affirmation of the vows of membership for those seeking to become members.

How high is that threshold for prospective new members in your church?

The high-threshold congregations often operate on the assumption that their primary responsibility is to transform people's lives. Nonbelievers are persuaded to become believers and to accept Jesus Christ as their personal Lord and Savior, and believers are transformed into disciples of Jesus Christ.

The low-threshold churches tend to focus on responding

"Jesus had such great expectations of his disciples that today we call most of them 'saints!'"

—FRIAR TUCK

to the religious and social needs of adults and their children. Their emphasis often is on transmitting the central teachings of the Christian faith, rather than on transforming the lives of individuals.

THE MORE I GIVE *of* MYSELF THE MORE *of* MYSELF HAVE I TO GIVE *!*

CHURCH SPONSORED BLOOD DRIVE TODAY!

—FRIAR TUCK

Churches with high expectations create folks who are saintly exceptions!

Does your congregation focus primarily on transmitting information? Or on transforming people's lives? Is a low threshold or a high threshold for membership the compatible way to undergird that emphasis? (It should be noted here that critics who carry a powerful European religious heritage fear that the road to Gnosticism is paved with stones bearing the word "REQUIRED." A current American response to that threat is to use the word "offer" rather than "require.")

A fourth way to reflect on this question is to measure direction. Is your congregation moving from a low-expectation style of ministry toward higher expectations from the members? Or is it drifting in the direction of lower expectations?

One indicator for measuring that is the worship attendance-to-membership ratio. The high-expectation churches usually report their weekend worship attendance is equivalent to at least 90 percent of their resident membership. In many that ratio is 200 or 300 or 400 percent. They welcome anyone who wants to worship with them and to participate in other ministries, but the threshold for membership is high. The middle-level expectation churches usually report that ratio is between 50 and 90 percent. The low-expectation churches report a ratio below 50 percent.

The reasons for placing this first among these self-evaluation questions include (a) the high-expectation churches are more likely to produce high-commitment members than are low-expectation churches and (b) to a significant degree this represents the self-fulfilling prophecy. The congregations that deliberately project high expectations of people tend to become high-commitment churches. Those that project modest expectations tend to attract the people who prefer a low-commitment church.

Uninformed critics of these high-commitment churches sometimes confuse the issue by identifying them as highly legalistic or fundamentalist or as cults. This is far from accurate. A classic example of a legalistic approach to this subject came in 1610, when the colonial legislature in Virginia adopted a three-level series of penalties for failure to attend Sunday morning worship. One failure to attend was punished with forfeiture of one week's provisions. Skipping church twice was punished by a whipping. The punishment for three unexcused absences was death.[2]

In today's highly permissive society, legalisms are not effective motivators except in a few ultraconservative religious traditions.[3] The vast majority of today's high-commitment churches are organized not around legalisms but around expectations, and they frequently

WHEW! I MAY BE RUNNING LATE, BUT AT LEAST I'M ALIVE!

DING! DONG!

—FRIAR TUCK.

In 1610 Virginia, three unexcused absences from church could result in the death penalty!

use the word "offer" rather than the word "require." A twentieth-century example was the congregation that expected every member to participate in public worship every Sunday morning and also offered Sunday evening worship for those who wanted to worship God twice every Sunday. People, both members and constituents, are expected to take the teachings of Jesus seriously. These churches expect that the life of the believer will be transformed by accepting Jesus Christ as Lord and Savior. These churches expect believers to live out their faith. That is one reason so many people from high-commitment churches volunteer to feed the hungry, to spend a few weeks working in a mission post on another continent, to shelter the homeless, to return their tithe to the Lord via that congregation, to pray for others, to be engaged in a serious and continuing study of the Scripture, to visit those in jail, to help plant new missions, to express compassion toward those in need, to attend an adult class while their children are in Sunday school rather than to gather in a corner to drink coffee and talk, to invite others to come to their church, to welcome strangers, to make substantial personal sacrifices in support of the ministry of their church, and to witness to their faith in their place of work.

Those factors explain why this question is placed first on this list of self-appraisal concerns. What are the expectations your congregation projects of people? Are these expectations the same for nonbelievers, occasional visitors, believers, and disciples?

B. Who Is Our Number One Constituency?

A second useful congregational self-evaluation yardstick is generated by the advice repeatedly given to manufacturers, publishers, retailers, health care professionals, colleges, owners of service agencies, salespeople, teachers, writers, producers of television programs, and many others. That advice is "Know your customer!" The old approach to marketing was to focus on the needs of the seller. The new approach focuses on the needs of the consumer.[4] The old approach encouraged the seller to "push his product." The new approach requires a far greater sensitivity to the needs of the buyer.

For congregational self-evaluation, this question begins with asking who is our number one constituency? Why do we exist? What are we trying to do?

Are we pushing our product or responding to the needs of others?
—FRYAR TUCK

Typical responses include: "Please God!" "Worship God," "Evangelize the world," "Serve the people living in this neighborhood," "Care for our members," "Help to support our denomination," "Maintain a Christian witness in this community," and "Perpetuate the traditions and ministry of our church in this community."

One long-range planning committee concluded, "We were created to serve the immigrants from the Netherlands who were establishing a colony here in this part of Michigan. That was our first constituency. We identified a second constituency in 1893 when we became the first and only Reformed Dutch Church in this city to worship God in English. In 1953 we defined a new constituency when we relocated the meeting place to reach and serve the families moving into this new residential community. Since 1975 we have been growing older and fewer in numbers as we focus increasingly on the needs of our members. The boats no longer are coming over from the Netherlands, and the time has come for us to identify our constituency for the early years of the twenty-first century."

In another congregation the planning committee members decided, "Since the law of our denomination states that the first claim on every dollar anyone places in the offering place is to pay the salary of our minister, it appears our number one customer is our pastor."

Do your priorities reflect your members, staff, or the unchurched in your community?

What drives the decision-making processes in your congregation? For whom is that weekend schedule of worship and teaching designed? As we express our priorities in our budget, who are the leading constituents? The members? The staff? The building? Our denomination? The unchurched people in this community? Children? Youth? Couples with children at home? Mature adults? Single parents? Recent immigrants from Asia?

In southern California a Japanese Baptist congregation was founded in 1925. By 1977 the average worship attendance had shrunk to thirty-five. After an agonizing self-appraisal, the congregation redefined its constituency from Japanese Americans to Asian Americans, relocated the meeting place, and by 1996 was averaging more than a thousand at worship.

A meaningful self-evaluation process may begin by identifying the two or three current major constituencies of that congregation. The second step may be to agree on the identity of potential new constituents. Can we increase the number of our potential constituents? The third step calls for a realistic definition of the religious and personal needs of these constituencies, both old and new. The often painful fourth step requires an accurate appraisal of the relevance and quality of how this congregation is responding to those needs.

A different response to this question can be summed up in these terms. This is the slice of the population who live within a ten- (twenty-) mile radius of our meeting place that we now serve. These are their general characteristics. Are we content with the size and the boundaries of that slice? Or should we attempt to penetrate that slice deeper by reaching more people who fit into that slice? Or should we try to reach and serve a wider slice of the population? Or should we launch some new off-campus ministries to reach slices of the population who probably would never come to our meeting place?[5]

A common pattern is represented by Old First Church meeting in a building on a 12,000 square foot lot in the central business section of this city of 15,000 residents. In 1950 the membership was 1,800 and nearly all the members lived within the corporate boundaries of the city. The combination of (a) the erosion of inherited institutional loyalties, (b) the widespread ownership of private motor vehicles, (c) the organization of many new congregations, (d) the replacement of neighborhood institutions (grocery stores,

> YES . . .
> WE'RE OPEN at 1 A.M.,
> SINCE WE KNEW
> THAT'S WHEN
> YOU'D BE GETTING IN!

—FRIAR TUCK

For whom is your weekend schedule of worship and teaching designed?

doctor's offices, gasoline stations, hardware stores, hospitals, churches, banks, and so forth) by large regional institutions, (e) the suburbanization of the population, and (f) the change in the sources of friendship ties in building one's personal social network has increased the competition among the churches for members born after 1955.

Today, with a membership of 735, Old First Church has five basic alternatives, (1) concentrate on serving a shrinking and aging membership, (2) relocate and become a large regional church, (3) sharply raise the quality and relevance of its ministry and broaden the scope as it becomes a seven-day-a-week church, (4) purchase adjacent property and become a regional church at this site, or (5) expand off-campus ministries.

C. What Is Our Niche?

Overlapping that second question is one some will find more comfortable. As recently as the 1950s thousands of congregations enjoyed a precisely defined niche in the local ecclesiastical marketplace. This congregation was a German Lutheran parish. Another was the only black congregation in town. Over there is the church that once included many of the movers and shakers in this city. That was a Swedish Baptist church. Over there is the meeting place of a Scotch Presbyterian congregation. That open country church was composed almost entirely of farmers and retired farmers. This was a neighborhood church that drew most of its members from within a two-mile radius. That was the only Pentecostal church in this part of the county. That was the only church in town with a full-time choir director, and its distinctive niche was classical music. That was the church for the blue collar workers in the mill, and up on the hill was the church the white collar workers and the bosses attended. That is a Norwegian Lutheran parish.

The passage of time, the automobile, the Americanization of the immigrant population, the erosion of denominational loyalties, the sharp decrease in the farm population, the impact of denominational mergers, the softening of social class lines, the increase in interdenominational and interfaith marriages, and other changes have wiped out the distinctive niche enjoyed by many congregations.

Concurrently a huge variety of new niches have evolved that reinforce the distinctive identity of particular congregations. This can be illustrated by looking at a dozen examples.

1. The ministry with the recently widowed members. Very, very few congregations provide an effective ministry with recently widowed women under age forty-five or with widowed men. In the average week approximately 20,000 marriages are terminated by the death of one spouse. One result is that the American population now includes 10 million currently widowed women and 2 million currently widowed men. This can be a highly redemptive and unique ministry for the congregation that includes many widowed persons as the foundation on which to build.

WHO SAYS THAT THERE'S NO ONE OUT THERE WHO NEEDS US?

—FRIAR TUCK

In an average week, about 20,000 marriages end in the death of a spouse!

2. Another choice is a ministry built around music and young children. This special niche can draw people

from a huge radius as the program that enables young children to express their creativity and to communicate through music, especially instrumental music. This requires a leader with special training in that field.

3. Overlapping that is a larger niche for those congregations that both promise, and have mobilized the resources to fulfill the promise, "We'll help you raise your children." Typically this includes special classes for new parents on how to appropriately intellectually stimulate babies, a prekindergarten weekday program for three- and four-year-olds, music programming for children ages one to three, parenting classes, adult Sunday school classes for single parents, summer camping experiences, marriage enrichment weekends, and similar specialized programing.[6]

4. A growing number of churches have found a special niche in a ministry with families that include a developmentally disabled child.

5. Several smaller congregations have built a unique niche by challenging people, especially mature adults, to be engaged in ministry with others. This may include the annual work camp mission trip to another country or a crew that helps construct the first meetinghouse for new congregations or a partnership with a nearby nursing home or children's home or elementary school.

6. A rapidly growing number of congregations have carved out a new niche, often following the arrival of a pastor in his or her second marriage, in building a ministry with couples who are in their second or subsequent marriage.

7. While this has been limited largely to congregations averaging fewer than a hundred at worship, dozens of churches have found a clearly identified niche as a

church organized around peace or world hunger or some other social action focus.

8. Back in the 1970s dozens of congregations carved out a very distinctive niche by welcoming "the Jesus people." Others became the home for a local expression of the Charismatic Renewal movement or a parachurch movement.

9. One of the more popular niches is to become a learning community. Many expressions of this concept exist, but most require excellent teachers and are high-expectation congregations.

10. One of the great unmet needs is to provide a warm and supportive church home for the rapidly growing number of single parent families.

11. A growing number of congregations have responded to the increasing number of parents who seek a small, high quality, and avowedly Christian day school for their children.

12. Several dozen congregations, most of them averaging fewer than 150 people at worship, have emerged as truly multicultural or racially integrated churches and identified that as their special niche.

Our Niche...

What makes your church unique?

—FRIAR TUCK

In addition to the central role as a worshiping community, has your church carved out a distinctive niche in ministry that helps to define its identity in the larger community? If not, has the time come to do that?

D. How Large Is Our Parish?

The 1950s brought a radical redefinition of the service area of churches. For 350 years, it was widely assumed that churches should serve the people living within a mile or two of that congregation's meeting place. That definition of the constituency was often sharpened by references to language, national origins, race, income, education, social class, denominational affiliation, occupation, and theological stance.

Seven revolutionary changes have undermined that concept of the geographical definition of a congregation's constituency. The first was Henry Ford's dream of manufacturing automobiles that working-class people could afford. The second was the ecumenical movement that encouraged Christians to focus on what they shared in common rather than on what divided them. A third was television that raised people's expectations about what they were entitled to out in the marketplace. A fourth was the erosion of inherited institutional loyalties. A fifth, and perhaps the most significant, was the redefinition of the foundation for building social networks from one's place of residence to one's vocation or one's personal needs. The sixth was the decision by the generations born after 1940 to move relevance, quality, credibility, and choices ahead of denominational loyalties, geographical convenience, kinship ties, nationality, ethnic heritages, tradition, and congregational loyalties in choosing a church home. The seventh was that rapid increase in interdenominational, interracial, and interfaith marriages.

Together these seven changes have greatly increased the level of competition among congregations for new members to replace the people who have left.

In somewhat oversimplified terms this leaves most congregations with four choices.

1. Carve out a distinctive, clearly defined, and highly visible niche.
2. Become the best and highest quality "community church" in that community.
3. Accept the role as a regional church serving people living within a five- or ten- or twenty- or thirty-mile radius of the meeting place. (Typically a five-mile radius will include six or seven times as many residents as a two-mile radius.)

Growing churches emphasize relevance, quality, and credibility over family, nationality, geographic, and denominational loyalty!
—FRIAR TUCK

4. Watch passively as your members grow older in age and fewer in number.

Which of these four alternatives comes closest to describing your congregation today? Has the time come to enlarge the geographical definition of your parish?

E. What Is Our Approach to Ministry?

"What does our minister do best? That's an easy question," replied a leader at the 168-member St. Paul Church. "Our pastor is a good preacher and an excellent teacher, but when you ask for the number one gift, that has to be one-to-one relationships. Our current pastor is better at one-to-one relationships than any minister I've ever met."

"We need to add someone to our staff, perhaps on a part-time basis, who can expand the small group life of this con-

I GUESS THIS IS WHAT I DO BEST!

FRIAR TUCK CARTOONS

—FRIAR TUCK—

Is it preaching, teaching, administration, or pastoral care that your pastor does best?

gregation," declared the minister at the 385-member Central Church. "I can handle the preaching, the administration, and most of the other pastoral work, but I simply do not have the time necessary to organize and nurture the small groups we need here."

"While it's true we don't find our current pastor to be an inspiring leader, and his sermons leave a lot of room for improvement, we couldn't leave if we wanted to," commented a member of the 760-member Bethel Church. "I not only sing in the chancel choir, I also direct one of the children's choirs. My husband is superintendent of the Sunday school, and my mother, who moved in with us six years ago, has found a home in the women's fellowship. Our seventeen-year-old is president of the youth choir, and our thirteen-year-old loves the junior high group."

"Why did we pick this church when we live fourteen miles away?" replied the forty-three-year-old husband who was a recent new member at the 945-member First Church. "I can answer your questions with one word. Program. This church offers the range and quality in programming our family was seeking when we moved here nearly two years ago. We visited at least a dozen churches during those first four months, but this is the only church we found that has the program we want."

"I joined this congregation twenty-five years ago because of its active support of the civil rights movement," recalled a member of the 113-member Emmanuel Church. "We've always been on the cutting edge of the issues of the day, and now we're spearheading the peace movement in this area. We're convinced the world has never needed the prophetic voice of the Christian faith more than it needs it today."

"For as long as I can remember, I've always considered myself to be a Christian," explained a leader at Trinity Church, "but it wasn't until after I started coming here that I understood the distinction between being a believer and living one's life as a disciple of Jesus Christ. This is a church that persuades skeptics, inquirers, doubters, seekers, searchers, and people on a self-identified religious pilgrimage to become believers. More important, in my opinion, it also challenges believers to become disciples."

"My wife and I have been members of seven different churches since we were married," declared a sixty-one-year-old man. "At one time or another, I've been an elder, deacon, Sunday school teacher, treasurer, youth counselor, finance chairman, Bible teacher, president of the men's fellowship, board member, usher, church softball team player, greeter, and about every other volunteer job you can expect a layman to fill. Four months after we joined this church, however, I was asked to be part of a three-person team to go out and start a new Sunday school for kids living in a public housing apartment building. Six months later we had thirty kids and nearly a dozen adults enrolled in the Sunday school that met in the community building. Our next step was to work with the residents in creating a new worshiping community there. We now have fifty regular attenders in the Sunday school, and the church service averages about forty in attendance. Two of the residents and I take turns doing the preaching, and four other residents, along with one member of our team, serve as the worship team. Our hope is that within a year the three of us will be able to disengage ourselves and this will be a self-expressing, self-governing, self-propagating, and self-financing congregation completely staffed by residents of that building."

These foregoing responses represent seven very different approaches to organizing the life and ministry of a worshiping community. These seven examples also introduce a different beginning point for congregational self-appraisal.

1. What is your approach to ministry?
2. Is it built around a network of one-to-one relationships with that personable, gregarious, and caring pastor at the hub?
3. Is it an organization of organizations, fellowships, classes, choirs, cells, circles, groups, and committees?
4. Is it largely organized around worship?
5. Is it primarily organized as a network of attractive programs?
6. Is it primarily organized around the magnetic personality of an exceptionally competent preacher?
7. Is it basically organized as a network of small groups?
8. Is it primarily organized to rally like-minded people around a social justice agenda?
9. Is it organized around the goal of offering people a huge array of attractive choices in worship, learning, music, groups, volunteer involvement in ministry, and outreach?
10. Is it largely organized around supporting and implementing denominational goals?
11. Is it primarily organized to enlist, train, and empower the laity to do ministry?
12. Is it primarily organized to care for today's members and to transmit the Christian faith to their children?

The self-appraisal process might include these three steps: (1) add to that list of alternative approaches or central organizing principles, (2) agree on what is number one, number two, and number three for your congregation today, and

(3) discuss whether or not you are satisfied with those three being at the top of the list.

F. What Do We Do Best?

Somewhere among the first several questions to be raised in this sequence is a highly subjective issue with two facets. In simple terms it is an appraisal of assets and liabilities. The temptation often is to begin by building a litany of weaknesses and liabilities. "Our building is functionally obsolete." "We can't find competent and committed volunteers." "We only have six off-steet parking spaces." "Our pastor is unhappy here and wants to move." "We only have a handful of children in our Sunday school."

THEY'RE THE "IN GOOD HANDS PEOPLE"!

—FRIAR TUCK

What one strength is the cohesive force in _your_ parish?

While those complaints reflect real concerns that cannot be ignored, a healthier beginning point is to identify strengths and assets that can be the foundation for building a new tomorrow. To be more specific, before identifying liabilities, it may be useful to ask these seven questions.

1. What do we do best in ministry?
2. What is the best new ministry we have launched during the past three years?
3. What does our pastor (staff) do best? What are their special gifts, skills, and competencies that can be the basis for expanding our ministry?

4. Where would it be easiest to raise the quality of what we offer?
5. What are the unique gifts and skills of our volunteer leaders on which we can build?
6. What do we do effectively here that is relatively concealed and that we should lift up to greater visibility, both for the benefit of our present members as well as potential future members?
7. What are the advantages that we enjoy because of the location of our meeting place?

G. What Is Our Driving Motivation?

In a great oversimplification of the real ecclesiastical world, all Protestant congregations in North America are organized around one of three central driving forces. That driving force is the number one factor in making major decisions. They are (1) institutional survival, (2) congregation-building, and (3) Kingdom-building.

A reasonable estimate is that well over one-half of all Protestant congregations on the North American continent that were established before 1975 fit into that first category. Institutional survival is the most influential force in their decision-making processes. While this tends to be most common in the one-half that average fewer than seventy-five at worship, many larger congregations are driven by survival goals. This often is reflected in the allocation of financial resources, in the responsibilities assigned the most competent volunteers, in the priorities on the pastor's time, and in the schedule. It also is reflected in a piece of conventional wisdom occasionally given to new ministers, "If you take care of your people, they will take care of you."

Another 30 to 40 percent of all congregations fit into the second category of congregation-building. The highest priorities are given to those actions that will strengthen and expand the life and ministry of that worshiping community.

Perhaps 5 percent, maybe fewer, of all Protestant congregations on the North American continent are more concerned with building the kingdom of God than with strengthening and expanding their congregations. The distinction between the second and the third categories can be illustrated by reflecting on eight frequently heard comments.

As one-half of all Protestant churches now focus on institutional survival, they're finding fewer and fewer defenders within!
—FRIAR TUCK

1. "If we expect to reach younger adults, we need to add a nontraditional worship service built around contemporary Christian music to our Sunday morning schedule!"
2. "When we decided to relocate to a larger site, we sold the old property to a Greek Orthodox congregation. That guaranteed that none of our longtime members who loved the building would be tempted to switch to the congregation who purchased it."
3. "We pay our pastor about $7,500 a year more than most ministers of the same age and experience level in this size congregation. We do this because we are very happy with our present pastor and because we know how disruptive pastoral changes can be. If and when our pastor leaves us, we want it to be in response to a call from God, not for more money."
4. "Recently we added a full-time person to our paid

staff to work with high school youth with a special emphasis on reaching kids who do not go to any church."

5. "Our goal is to help start at least one new congregation every year."

6. "When we relocated to a twenty-acre site seven miles away, we sold the old property to a new independent congregation that reaches approximately the same slice of the population that we serve. One result is nearly 300 of our members decided to switch their membership to this new independent church and stay with the building they helped plan and pay for several years ago. We affirm their decision!"

7. "The first thirty cents out of every dollar in the offering plate goes to missions."

8. "Three times a year we run two optional two-hour events for our members who are moving away. The first is designed to help them formulate the criteria they will use in finding a new church. The second event is designed to enhance their skills in becoming active members of that congregation."

What are the common threads running through those statements? The first four were articulated by leaders who can be described as primarily congregation-builders. Their number one goal is to strengthen their congregation. They are to be affirmed and commended! We have a national shortage of committed Christians who are dedicated to enhancing the vitality, strength, evangelistic outreach, relevance, and quality of their congregation.

The second four statements came from congregational leaders who are committed to strengthening their church, but their number one characteristic is they are Kingdom-builders. Their number one goal is to help build and extend the kingdom of God. They also are to be affirmed and commended! Their numbers, however, are much smaller than the number of congregation-builders.

With but one big exception, the congregation-builders closely resemble the Kingdom-builders. That big exception is the choice of a benchmark or criterion for making decisions. When a specific polity question is raised, the congregation-builder asks, "How will this affect my congregation?" The Kingdom-builder asks, "How will this strengthen or enlarge the kingdom of God?"

While the number of laypersons in congregations on the North American continent outnumber the clergy by approximately a four hundred-to-one ratio, the laity who are primarily Kingdom-builders may outnumber the clergy who are primarily Kingdom-builders by only a five-to-one or ten-to-one ratio.

This should not be perceived as an either-or line of demarcation. The key word is "primarily." Is that person's focus *primarily* on congregation-building or *primarily* on Kingdom-building? Many leaders in the churches are concerned about *both* congregation-building *and* Kingdom-building. The pivotal question is which is their primary concern?

Who? What is our driving motivation?

Finally, for those who are nervous around leaders who are eager to build their own private personal empire or kingdom, relax! That is another subject. This is about building the kingdom of God, not about creating a personal fiefdom.

What is the primary driving force in how major decisions are made in your congregation? Institutional survival? Congregation-building? Kingdom-building?

H. What Do We Expect of Our Pastor and Staff?

One of the most widely used metaphors to describe the role and work of a parish pastor is the term "shepherd." Among the New Testament references for this term are the repeated analogies used in the tenth chapter of the Gospel of John. "He calls his own sheep by name and leads them out" (John 10:3). "The good shepherd lays down his life for the sheep" (John 10:11). This was and continues to be a useful analogy for the pastor of the small congregation in which the minister is expected to feed the spiritual hunger of the members of that flock and to care for them.[7]

OF COURSE, IT'S LONELY UP HERE, BUT AT LEAST I CAN SEE WHAT'S COMING!

—FRIAR TUCK.

A reliable source for a vision of tomorrow can be the pastor!

One of the most significant changes in American Christianity during the past 100 years has been the emergence of larger congregations.[8] The average (mean) size of Roman Catholic parishes in the United States quintupled from 600 baptized members in 1890 to more than 3,000 in 1990. The average size of a Lutheran parish tripled from 143 baptized members in 1890 to 435 in 1990. The average size of a Presbyterian congregation also tripled from 95 members (all ages) in 1890 to 300 in 1990. The average size of an

Episcopal parish also tripled during that 100-year period from 106 baptized members to 333 in 1990. In most other American religious traditions the average size of a congregation doubled or tripled during that 100-year period.

EVERYTHING IN OUR CHURCHES WILL BE ON HOLD UNTIL...

...we accept and affirm one another's primary concerns!

—FRIAR TUCK

That rapid growth raised the question, "How many sheep can one shepherd care for?" A common response was, "Not that many!" That often led to the addition of a second, or perhaps even a third or fourth pastor to the staff. Rather than change the metaphor, it was easier to increase the number of shepherds as the flock grew in size. That was consistent with a European religious tradition that placed the priest at the center of parish life.[9]

During the last three decades of the twentieth century, however, a radical new approach to ministry became increasingly common among American churches. In a landmark book, George Hunter III has described the "apostolic congregation" and how it reaches the people Hunter describes as in a "pre-Christian" stage of their pilgrimage. Hunter identified the ten features of an apostolic congregation. Four of the ten focus on trusting, enlisting, motivating, training, nurturing, and supporting lay volunteers in their involvement in ministries for which they are gifted.[10]

These apostolic congregations illustrate this radical new approach to ministry. Instead of hiring paid staff to do ministry on behalf of the gathered community, this new approach places

ANSWER: WE CAN NO LONGER AFFORD ANY OTHER OPTION!

NEW MODEL PASTOR
(PRICE LIST)
• HOUSING
• LIFE INSURANCE
• EXPENSES
• HOSPITALIZATION
• PENSION
• TRAVEL
• CONTINUING EDUCATION
• ETC.,
• ETC.,
• ETC.

—FRIAR TUCK—

Question: Why do we need to challenge and empower lay volunteers instead of adding clergy?

a far greater emphasis on challenging and empowering lay volunteers to do ministry. Another way to describe this issue is with a simple question: Does your congregation hire staff to be doers or trainers?

Most congregations choose to hire staff to do ministry. One congregation hires a youth minister. Another hires a part-time choir director. A third hires someone to call on all first- and second-time visitors to persuade them to join that church. A fourth hires a retired pastor to call on the hospitalized, the shut-ins, and the older members. A fifth hires an associate minister to do what the senior pastor (a) does not want to do or (b) cannot do. The more effective these hired staff persons, the bigger the hole they leave behind when eventually they do depart.

Two different approaches to staffing can be illustrated by the experiences of two different congregations. In the first, Pat McGuire, a trained lay specialist in Christian education, came to North Church in response to the plea to "build up our adult Sunday school."

Within two weeks after her arrival, Pat's first step was to organize and teach a challenging and in-depth adult Bible study program that met for two hours each Tuesday evening for two years. A total of twenty-seven adults enrolled, and two years later, nineteen graduated. Eight of those graduates then taught three weeknight Bible study groups. During the first three years on the job, Pat McGuire also organized and taught eight additional classes:

1. A thirteen-week class on methods in teaching adults that produced eight graduates committed to regular teaching responsibilities;

2. An eighteen-week class on the theology of evangelism that produced fourteen graduates;

3. An eighteen-week class trained five young mothers in a program designed to produce teachers for weekday Bible study groups for housewives. This produced five graduates. Two organized and led a Tuesday morning group and the other three led a Thursday morning group;

4. A ten-week class with five men who had been inspired by a PromiseKeepers weekend event and subsequently organized and led an early Saturday morning Breakfast and Bible Study group;

5. A sixteen-week Thursday evening class for parents who volunteered to teach classes on parenting that eventually produced two adult classes on parenting skills. One met on Tuesday evenings, and the other met during the Sunday school hour;

6. A thirty-six-week course on Christian interpersonal social skills that began with five single adults and by week thirty averaged nearly a hundred on Saturday mornings. Out of this group Pat chose five volunteers who organized and led the new singles' ministry that meets for three to five hours on Saturday evenings;

7. A thirteen-week class for engaged and recently married couples. Out of this class Pat chose three couples who organized and led a new Sunday school class for recently engaged couples and newlyweds. Six months later three other couples volunteered to organize and lead a new Sunday school class for couples with young children. A year later, with additional help from Pat, three other couples volunteered to organize and lead the new Phoenix class for couples

where one or both spouses were in their second or subsequent marriage;

8. A class of thirty-five adults, most of them born before 1940, who signed up for a thirty-two-week course that met during Sunday school. The first fifteen weeks were devoted to a study of the Holy Land. The next two weeks included a twelve-day trip, as part of a much larger professionally led tour group to Israel. The last fifteen weeks were reflections on what the participants had experienced and learned. Pat taught the first six weeks and accompanied the group on its trip. Volunteers led the class in other sessions and also provided the future leadership. What had begun as a loose collection of individuals evolved into a closely knit social network that insisted on continuing as an adult Sunday school class. At the end of three years, the number of adults engaged in serious, continuing weekly study had grown from an average attendance of twenty to well over 200, plus that Saturday evening singles' group that averaged close to 200 weekly.

Equally important, three years after her arrival, Pat had trained more than eighty volunteers actively involved as leaders or teachers in the adult teaching ministries at North Church. After four years, in the typical week this energetic and visionary staff member could report approximately 500 adults engaged in one form or another of structured, serious, and ongoing learning experiences at North Church.

Pat McGuire's work produced six other benefits for this congregation. First, what had been a "one hour on Sunday morning" low-commitment congregation became a mid- to high-commitment church. The new expectation was that everyone be present for at least two periods of time on Sunday morning. A growing array of high quality, relevant,

and attractive adult classes led by trained teachers reinforced that higher expectation.

Second, the attractive learning experiences for adults, plus
the work of the graduates from that theology of evangelism
class, combined as central factors for a 50 percent worship-
attendance increase in six years.

Third, in these training events McGuire emphasized not
only high expectations in competence but also self-esteem
and self-confidence. This boosted the morale of all the
teachers and eventually encouraged the other volunteers at
North Church.

Fourth, the teaching ministries, including the training
events, became the number one channel for the assimilation
of newcomers into the larger fellowship of North Church.

Fifth, this increase in members and in the adult Sunday
school led to a 60 percent increase in attendance in the children's and youth Sunday school classes.

Sixth, and perhaps most
important of all, these learning experiences greatly enriched the personal and spiritual life of all who partic-
ipated.

A different style was dis-
played by The Reverend
Martha Green, the first full-
time associate minister at
Bethany Church.

As the first full-time associate minister, Martha was
free of any expectations created by a predecessor. In
those earlier interviews with
the pulpit nominating committee and the pastor, Martha

GRUNT!!

MANY ARE CALLED,
BUT FEW CHOOSE...

—FRIAR TUCK

... the faith and
effort of becoming
a highly committed church!

had made it clear that her number one interest would be in creating high quality training experiences for volunteers.

During her first three years, Martha found three residents of the community who had been trained in the theory and practice of "music and movement-based learning." Martha enlisted them, plus a music teacher from a nearby college, to train sixteen parents in how to appropriately stimulate the intellectual development of babies and young children. Subsequently three of those parents volunteered to offer a twenty-week class for prospective new parents.

One cf the assets Martha inherited were three volunteers who had been trained as leaders in the Stephen Series for caregivers. Two of those Stephen leaders, with the help of a member who is a pastoral counselor, plus a physician, two specialists from the local hospital, and a member who is a nurse-practitioner, created a fifty-session program to train volunteers to make hospital calls. About half were generalists and half were specialists. The specialists consisted of people with distinctive personal experiences. Mothers who had given birth by a cesarean procedure were trained to call on mothers who were about to give birth by a cesarean section. Ditto for persons who had survived surgery for cancer of the colon or a heart bypass operation and other difficult surgical procedures.

Three years after her arrival Martha and the senior pastor could brag to their ministerial friends, "At Bethany, 95 percent of all hospital calls are made by trained lay volunteers."

Martha also created training programs for (a) widows and widowers to minister with the recently widowed, (b) persons who are divorced to minister with those experiencing a painful divorce, (c) parents with adopted children to minister with those contemplating adoption, (d) producing the local leadership required to create new prayer groups for men after they returned from a PromiseKeepers weekend, (e) volunteers to teach high-expectation adult Bible study groups, (f) volunteers who agreed to help staff ministries with families that include teenagers, (g) volunteers who would create the worship team required for the proposed new Saturday evening worship experience, and (h) what eventually became a cadre of forty volunteers who staffed a variety of ministries in off-campus locations including three nursing homes, a mobile home court, two low-income apartment communities, a shopping mall, and the local four-year liberal arts college.

Martha came into a congregation that was ready for an imaginative and energetic trainer. Martha did not see herself as "doing ministry." She saw her role as enlisting, challenging, motivating, training, nurturing, placing and supporting volunteers who would do ministry. She also did not see herself as *the* trainer. Her responsibility was to identify and enlist the people with the required specialized skills to be the trainers. At most, she did perhaps 10 percent of the actual training. She created and administered a wide variety of training programs.

By contrast, Pat McGuire came into a relatively passive congregation that had a long tradition of hiring people to do ministry.

While Martha Green can be described as a highly energetic facilitator, Pat McGuire is both a doer and a trainer. McGuire's first priority was to build up momentum, to project and fulfill the expectation that adult learning experiences can be and should be the norm at North Church. McGuire did that in those first three years by both teaching and training. During the second and third year her role and priorities gradually changed with an ever-increasing emphasis on overseeing, encouraging, supporting, nurturing, training volunteers, helping to give birth to new classes and groups, and counseling the doers. She accomplished this by shrinking her number of teaching hours. Initially Pat modeled the role of the enthusiastic, competent, trained, and self-confident

IT'S SIMPLE: WATCH ONE, DO ONE, TEACH ONE!

— FRIAR TUCK •

Training the laity instead of hiring clergy will be the ministry of the next millenium!

teacher. Five years later, North Church enjoyed the gifts and leadership of dozens of models of enthusiastic, competent, trained, and self-confident volunteer teachers and trainers.

While this is a plea to look for trainers, rather than simply doers, in recruiting new staff, three cautions must be raised. First, skilled trainers are rare and usually not inexpensive! Pat McGuire's total compensation in that eighth year was $48,000.

Second, and more important, the congregational context must be supportive of training. If the pastor prefers to "do it myself" over training volunteers, other staff members may find it difficult to be effective trainers. For obvious reasons, it is easier to build and maintain this focus on training if pastorates are for fifteen or twenty or more years than if they average three to seven years.

Third, the lower the commitment level of the congregation, the more difficult it will be to design and implement an effective training program. This focus on training works best in congregations that project high expectations of people. For example, if the ratio of worship attendance to confirmed membership is below 70 percent, it may be both tempting and easier to seek staff members who are productive doers rather than skilled trainers. For at least a few congregations the first priority may be to raise the commitment level. That can prepare the congregational culture for a high-expectation training program.

What has been the tradition of your congregation? To hire staff who will do ministry? Or to seek staff who will be both doers and trainers? Or to place training ahead of doing as your plan for meeting staff needs? What should be the top priority as you enter the third millennium?

CHAPTER TWO

What Do the Numbers Tell Us?

O LORD, I WISH YOU'D ANSWER MY PRAYERS WITH MORE OBJECTIVE DATA!

—FRIAR TUCK.

Like our faith walk with god, our appraisal of churches is hardly explainable and quantifiable!

A t least a few of the leaders in any effort at congregational self-appraisal will become impatient with the subjective nature of the eight questions presented in the first chapter. These leaders want hard facts. They look for quantifiable yardsticks. They will not be satisfied with anything less than measurable objective data. That is a legitimate demand. Numbers can be useful. They are especially useful in (a) defining significant trends in congregational life, (b) comparing one congregation with others, and (c) identifying what the congregational or denominational leaders perceive to be important by looking at what they measure. The eleven questions in this

58

chapter can be a useful part of that self-appraisal process in most congregations.

A. How Large Is This Congregation?

Perhaps the best beginning point for the statistical phase of congregational self-appraisal is to look at the size of the congregation. The absence of any uniformity in the definition of the term "member" means that criterion often is somewhere between useless and misleading. A far better yardstick for measuring size is the average worship attendance. Ideally this will reflect the number of people of all ages who are present for the entire worship service. The average for the year becomes a useful number for comparison purposes.

The first comparison can be with the median for your denomination. The median is the number in an array that represents the middle. For example, the median average worship attendance in The United Methodist Church in 1974 was sixty-one. That meant that one-half of the congregations in that denomination reported an average worship attendance of sixty-one or fewer and one-half reported their average worship attendance was more than sixty-one. By 1995 the median in that denomination had dropped to fifty-six. The accompanying table reports the median average worship attendance in several other denominations.

Median Average Worship Attendance 1994

Denomination	Median Average Attendance
American Baptist Churches	80
Assemblies of God	70
Baptist General Conference	105
Church of the Brethren	58
Church of the Nazarene	65
Disciples of Christ	75
Evangelical Covenant Church	98
Evangelical Free Church	115
Evangelical Lutheran Church in America	100
Free Methodist Church	55
Lutheran Church-Missouri Synod	124
Presbyterian Church (U.S.A.)	75
National Association of Congregational Christian Churches	60
Reformed Church in America	114
Southern Baptist Convention	71
United Church of Christ	72
The United Methodist Church	56
Wesleyan Church	56
Wisconsin Evangelical Lutheran Synod	92

A second comparison figure is derived from the fact that on the typical weekend well over one-half of the people worshiping with a Protestant congregation in the United States can be found in 15 percent of the congregations. It also should be noted that the churchgoers born before 1940 can be found in disproportionately large numbers in smaller congregations while the churchgoers born after 1955 are worshiping in disproportionately large numbers in the

Alas, the smaller the church, the older its congregation seems to be!

larger churches. This suggests that by the year 2025 at least one-half of all Protestant churchgoers will be worshiping in only 10 percent of the churches. Is your congregation among that largest 10 percent in size? In statistical terms that would be the ninety-first through the hundreth percentile. The accompanying table reports the ninetieth percentile in average worship attendance for nineteen denominations.

If your congregation exceeds that number, it probably ranks in the top 10 percent in size in your denomination.

In addition to the relative size, look at the trend. Has the average worship attendance in your congregation been increasing? If yes, gradually or rapidly? Why? Has it been declining? If yes, gradually or rapidly? Why?

It is not unusual for year-to-year fluctuations to run between 2 and 3 percent. If, however, the year-to-year changes (a) are all in the same direction and (b) total more than 15 percent over

the past five years, it is important to ask two questions. First, why? Second, what are the probable implications?

For example, during the past five years, the average worship attendance at the Oak Hill Church rose from 150 to 180, an increase of 20 percent. This has moved that congregation out of what often is one of the two most comfortable size brackets (the other is an average worship attendance of thirty-five to forty) in American Protestantism into what has been described as the *awkward size* congregation.[1] How will this growth affect our staffing needs? Has the time come to expand the schedule to two worship services on Sunday morning? Or is the growth largely a product of that expansion of the schedule? Will we need more space to accommodate that many more people? Can we assimilate the newcomers if our growth curve continues at this pace? Have we been able to enlist the appropriate number of new members in policy-making positions? These are only a few of the questions evoked by that rate of increase.

More common is the congregation that reports a decrease from 150 to 120 in average worship attendance over five years, also a change of 20 percent. Is that a product of a shrinking population in this community? Or a change in the characteristics of the population? Or a mismatch between the needs of that congregation and the gifts of that minister? Or does that drop in attendance simply reflect the continua-

90th Percentile
in Average Worship Attendance

American Baptist Churches	250
Assemblies of God	240
Baptist General Conference	335
Church of the Brethren	154
Church of the Nazarene	187
Disciples of Christ	210
Evangelical Covenant Church	325
Evangelical Free Church	400
Evangelical Lutheran Church in America	290
Free Methodist Church	175
Lutheran Church-Missouri Synod	355
National Association of Congregational Christian Churches	185
Presbyterian Church (U.S.A.)	245
Reformed Church in America	390
Southern Baptist Convention	255
United Church of Christ	201
United Methodist Church	258
Wesleyan Church	170
Wisconsin Evangelical Lutheran Synod	225

...can denote a trend!

—FRIAR TUCK

Are your year-to-year changes all tilting in the same direction?

—FRIAR TUCK

tion of a long-term shrinkage in size? Or is this congregation no longer competitive in reaching younger generations of churchgoers? Or is it a signal that the time has come to redefine the role of this congregation?

A third example is the congregation that experienced an increase in average worship attendance from 180 five years ago to nearly 300 today. That growth has moved it out of the middle-sized church category into the large church bracket. Is everyone ready to affirm that the time has come to act like a big church? Are the members of the governing board ready to move from a rationing role into a planning-for-a-new-tomorrow perspective?

B. What Is the Ratio?

The key variable in this next question is the definition of membership. The question appears to be relatively simple. What is the ratio of the average worship attendance-to-resident membership, age fourteen and over? In high-expectation churches (see question A in chapter 1) that ratio usually runs above 90 percent.

The limitation in this question is in the definition of membership. Some congregations have a high threshold for becoming and continuing as a full member while in other churches that is a very low threshold. Therefore it may be useful to compare that ratio with the ratio of worship attendance-to-membership for all the churches in your denomination or in your regional judicatory.

For most congregations, however, a revealing follow-up question asks, Has that ratio been going up or down over the past few years? Why? What are the probable implications?

C. What Is the Median Tenure?

This often is among the two or three most revealing statistical indicators for that congregational self-appraisal

AH YES, THERE ARE NO STRANGERS *in* PARADISE!

— FRIAR TUCK

In high-expectation, growing churches, 90% of its members attend weekly worship!

HOW DOES YOUR CHURCH DEFINE MEMBERSHIP?

- TITHER
- REGULAR VOLUNTEER
- NINETY-PERCENT ATTENDER
- CHURCH SCHOOL TEACHER
- PRAYS, READS BIBLE DAILY

— FRIAR TUCK

GETTING THEM HERE WAS NO PROBLEM! GETTING THEM IN WILL BE!

Today, it's often easier to attract new members than assimilate them!
—FRIAR TUCK

GULP! THE OLDER WE GET, THE LESS LIKELY WE'LL ATTRACT OR KEEP YOUNGER MEMBERS!

EXIT

—FRIAR TUCK

effort. What is the median tenure of today's resident members? One-half of today's members joined before that date and one-half joined since that date. What is that date?

In the typical healthy congregation, that date usually is between eight and ten years earlier. If the median tenure is less than seven years ago, it raises two questions. First, is this a new congregation formed less than a dozen years ago? If so, that explains it. Second, if this congregation was launched more than twenty years earlier, can it assimilate that many newcomers this rapidly? Frequently, it is easier to attract new members than it is to assimilate them.

If that date is more than twelve years ago, this raises three other questions. First, is the explanation that this congregation is composed largely of people who have passed their fiftieth birthday? Mature adults are less likely to change either their place of residence or their church affiliation than are younger adults. Second, is this simply a natural characteristic of the numerically shrinking congregation? Third, and most important, does it suggest this congregation has lost its capability to attract, welcome, and assimilate new members?

D. What Is the Frequency of Worship Attendance?

"Our church attendance has dropped by nearly a third in the past two years," commented a member of First Church, "and I don't understand it. We've been receiving more new members every year than we lose, but our attendance has been dropping."

"We've had just the opposite experience," replied a member from Trinity Church. "We've enjoyed a 10 percent increase in our worship attendance every year since our new minister came four years ago, but our confirmed membership total is down about 200. I guess that was largely a result of cleaning the membership rolls, however, and not an actual drop in the number of active resident members."

Nonmember Members

—FRIAR TUCK

"So what? So they aren't all members... It sure beats having pews to dust after church!"

"We've had the best of both worlds," boasted a member from Grace Church. "Our membership is 50 percent higher than it was seven years ago, and our church attendance also is up by almost 50 percent."

These comments illustrate four generalizations for those interested in congregational self-appraisal. First, only two possibilities exist to explain either a decrease or an increase in your worship attendance. One possibility is an increase in the number of different people who attend at least once over a period of several weeks. The second is an increase in the frequency of attendance. Those are the only roads open to increasing your attendance.

The second generalization is that an increase in one can be offset by a decrease in the other. Thus an increase in the number of people who attend at least once a month may not produce a net increase if a larger number of people who formerly rarely missed worship now attend only once or twice a month. Likewise, an increase in the number of those who rarely miss Sunday worship can be offset by a sharp drop in the total number of those who attend.

SORRY, BUT *the* ONLY TIME YOU CAN COUNT ON SEEING ME IS IN CHURCH ON SUNDAYS!

It's the folks who come most often who most likely will invite others!

FRIAR TUCK

The third generalization is that a successful effort to increase the frequency of attendance among today's members also may attract a substantial number of additional worshipers. One obvious reason is that an attractive worship experience not only tends to increase the frequency of attendance among the members, but also tends to cause first-time visitors and church shoppers to return. A second is that the member who attends fifty weekends a year is more likely to invite others to come to church than is the person who comes only five to ten Sundays a year.

The fourth generalization is that any strategy to increase worship attendance should include priorities. Is the top priority attracting more people? Or is the top priority increasing the frequency of attendance among today's members?

The first alternative will mean focusing your efforts and resources largely on people who do not now worship with you. The second alternative means placing your primary emphasis on a better response to the religious needs of your present constituency. Perhaps 5 percent of all Protestant congregations in North America have the resources that enable them to say that we will make both audiences a top priority.

Before reading further, it should be pointed out that compiling the data required for this step in self-appraisal is a BIG job! First, it requires a careful survey of worship attendance in order to gather the data. Normally this is done over four consecutive Sundays, preferably in October or late October and early November or in May. Those are the occasions when church attendance usually is neither much above nor much below the average for the year. One big exception, of course, consists of those congregations in the Sunbelt with large numbers of winter visitors during the first three months of the calendar year.

In those congregations with Saturday evening or Monday night or Saturday morning or Friday evening worship, the survey includes those services as well as Sunday morning.

The survey should produce these data:

1. Number of members at worship only once a month;
2. Number of members at worship two times;
3. Number of members at worship three times;
4. Number of members at worship four times;
5. Number of visitors attending once;
6. Number of visitors attending twice;
7. Number of visitors attending three times;
8. Number of visitors attending four times;
9. Average number of children who are not yet full members in worship each weekend;
10. The number of constituents who are not members who attend (a) once, (b) twice, (c) three times, or (d) four times.

It may be useful to ask each person present in worship to fill out a card listing name, zip code, year joined this church, and gender. One card should be filled out each week for each person present, regardless of age or marital status.

Among the questions to be addressed to this collection of data are these:

1. How many members were in worship only once or twice?
2. How many members were in worship three or four times?
3. How many resident members were not in worship even once?

In high-commitment congregations (see question A in chapter 1) the number of members in worship either three or four weekends will greatly exceed the number in worship only once or twice. In low-commitment churches, the number of members not attending even once in that four weekend period plus the number attending only once or twice often will be double the number of those attending on three or four weekends.

Similar analyses can be made on the frequency of attendance of visitors and constituents. The more attractive that congregation is to younger adults, the more likely that one-fourth to three-fourths of all attenders will be visitors and constituents (persons who attend regularly but choose not to join).

A second reason that this is a BIG undertaking is that it

helps to have a local benchmark. In other words, it is useful to carry out this attendance survey every October or every other October. That makes it possible to establish a trend line. Is the frequency of attendance of our members going up or down? Are we experiencing an increase in the number of visitors? In their frequency of attendance? Why?

What was the ratio of men to women among the regular attenders who were in worship at least three times during the survey period? A normal pattern is 53 percent adult women to 47 percent for adult men. When that ratio is 60 percent female and 40 percent male, it raises a question as to whether worship here is designed primarily for women. When that ratio moves up to 65-35, many more questions should be asked about why it is that way here. A common explanation is the worship experience is designed primarily for women. Another is an aging membership in which women outnumber men by a five-to-three ratio or a two-to-one ratio.

For this discussion we will assume the results of this survey reveal that the frequency of attendance is lower than is acceptable. What can you do about it? At least a dozen possibilities merit consideration, but note that several of these may not be appropriate for your congregation. If you conclude one of these is not appropriate, look at the next one. Do not waste time feeling guilty.

1. For some congregations the easiest way to increase worship attendance is to recognize that some people prefer to go to church early on Sunday morning while others prefer a later hour. Thus, in about four out of five cases, a shift from one worship experience on Sunday morning to two produces a 15 to 20 percent increase in attendance. In many congregations the building is too large to permit this unless it is renovated to make a small crowd feel comfortable in a big room.

298, 299, 300!...GET READY
PSSST! to GO ON!

If your attendance
averages over 300,
plan to add some kind of
instrumental group!
—FRIAR TUCK.

2. An alternative is to add another music group. If you now do not have a vocal choir, organize one. If you have one, add a second. If you regularly have two vocal choirs in the worship service, add an instrumental group. The younger your people and/or the larger proportion of worshipers who are newcomers and/or the larger the attendance and/or the greater the degree of anonymity among the people in the room, the more important is music. If you average over 300, add an instrumental group and maybe organize an orchestra or a band.

3. If your congregation includes many people who live alone, begin with breakfast.

4. If your present schedule consists of worship followed by Sunday school followed by worship, add an adult class at the first and/or last hour so adults can participate in an adult class, teach in the children's Sunday school, and also attend worship.

5. For many churches, the most effective means of increasing the frequency of worship attendance will be to improve the quality of the preaching. This may refer to sermon content or delivery or both. Television has raised people's expectations of what they can expect of anyone addressing large numbers of people. Or it may mean improving the content of the sermons.

Memorable sermons that speak in a meaningful way to people's spiritual needs can be the best way of increasing the frequency of attendance and also increasing the number of people who attend. How many of the sermons you heard last year stick in your memory?

6. Overlapping this is the sermon series. Too often the sermon series exists only in the head of the preacher. The influential sermon series causes this Sunday's worshipers to have one of two thoughts: *I wish I had been here last week*, or *I certainly intend to be here next Sunday!*

7. For low-commitment churches of all sizes, the most effective means of increasing attendance next Sunday is a pastoral visit this week. This can be made by a lay volunteer, but that visit should focus on the agenda of the person being called on, not on the agenda of the caller. The frequency of attendance often drops when people believe no one hears them or cares about what they think.

8. An increasing proportion of those larger congregations that have two or more ministers on the staff have found that the easiest way to increase the frequency of attendance is to have one minister preach at the early service forty-two Sundays a year and the other preach at the late service forty-two Sundays a year. This is more likely

to increase the frequency of attendance if (a) both ministers are excellent preachers and/or attractive personalities, (b) they do not rotate week by week, (c) each service includes an adult choir—but not the same choir for both services, and (d) the two services display substantial differences in format, choice of hymns and anthems, and each has has its own bulletin.

9. A growing number of churches are increasing the frequency of attendance by scheduling a wotship experience for that growing number of people who have to be at work on Sunday morning. This may be on Saturday evening or late Sunday afternoon or early Sunday evening or Monday evening. At least a couple of congregations are now experimenting with Saturday morning worship and a full educational offering.

10. Those with considerable patience argue the most effective way to increase the frequency of attendance is to raise expectations. Project the expectation that everyone is expected to share in corporate worship every Sunday. This may have the greatest immediate effect on tomorrow's new members. Some churches reinforce this with the requirement that no one can hold a volunteer office unless that person is a regular participant in worship.

11. Strengthen the adult Sunday school. This course of

action applies to churches of all sizes, but may have the most dramatic effect on (a) congregations averaging fewer than eighty-five at worship, (b) congregations seeking to reach adults born after 1945, and (c) churches averaging more than 700 at worship. Among other influences, attractive adult classes provide one more reason for people to get up and make the effort to go to church. The more reasons people have for coming to church, the higher the frequency of attendance.

12. Provide adequate and convenient off-street parking. Some readers will argue this should be higher on the list—and they may be right. The newer the congregation, the larger the attendance, the younger the people, and the larger the proportion of newcomers among the worshipers, the more important is convenient off-street parking. Likewise it tends to be more important west of Ohio than in New England and more important in the Southwest than in the Southeast. Ideally the congregation will own sixty off-street parking spaces for every 100 people who worship there on Sunday morning.

While this does not represent an exhaustive list of all possibilities, these are among the more widely used approaches to increasing the frequency of worship attendance. Which ones fit your situation?

E. What Is the Turnover Rate?

One of the most useful statistical tools in congregational self-appraisal is to examine the rate of turnover among the members. Prepare a table covering the past ten years, reporting on a year-by-year basis, the number of new members received and the number of members removed from the roll.

What is your turnover rate?

—FRIAR TUCK.)

HOW DO WE PROGRAM for A SURE EVALUATION?

ANALYSIS

—FRIAR TUCK.)

Membership retention and recruitment are usually the best criteria!

It may help to use several columns showing the number received by the various initiatory rituals such as baptisms, confirmation, and transfer, and a similar set for each subcategory for the removals.

An examination of the turnover rate in a congregation can be an informative exercise. First, it tells us how many replacements must be received to at least remain on a plateau in size.

Second, how does that compare with other churches? Typically the small rural congregation consisting largely of people who have passed their fiftieth birthday loses about 2 to 4 percent of their members annually. At the other end of that spectrum are the relatively new, very large, and exceptionally attractive congregations that include large numbers of single adults under thirty, many of whom had no previous active church affiliation for a decade or longer. It is not unusual for these churches to bid farewell to 30 to 40 percent of their people every year. Forty may leave in a typical month, but they are replaced by fifty newcomers.

The typical Protestant congregation in North America has to replace 6 to 10 percent of its members annually to remain on a plateau in size. If the focus is on ministries with husband-wife couples with teenage children, that rate may be closer to 5 to 7 percent. If the focus is on younger couples and single adults, it is more likely to be in the 9 to 12 percent range.

Third, what has been the trend over the past ten years? Why is the trend in that direction?

Fourth, this turnover table provides a basis for asking whether or not we are deluding ourselves. Frequently congregations add only the losses by death and by transfer in reporting the losses for the past year. When they neglect to report the number of members who have dropped into inactivity, some by moving away, this results in a misleading picture. It is not at all uncommon to read an annual report that shows a net increase in the membership when in fact the active membership declined. This delay in marking down the inventory of members may be reassuring to some and encourage denial, but it also can be very misleading. In simple terms, it offers a false baseline for planning and decision making.

Fifth, calculating the turnover rate every year provides one more piece of comparative data for a longer per-

GULP! A MEMBERSHIP TRANSFER IS JUST THE TIP *of* A CHILLING STATISTIC !

We need two or three new members for everyone who leaves!

—FRIAR TUCK,

spective. Is the death rate going up or down? What is the long-term trend in transfers out? How does the dropout rate compare with previous years?

Finally, the figures for losses offer a comparison base for looking at gains. On the average, for every two members who leave a Protestant church by letter of transfer, two others, exclusive of deaths, leave, but a letter of transfer is never requested. This means that the typical congregation must receive twice as many new members by letter of transfer as it loses by transfer if it is to remain on a plateau in size or it must receive an unusually large number of new members by profession of faith. (It should be noted that persons received on profession of faith or by adult baptism are far more likely to drop out than are persons received by letter of transfer.) On a long-term basis, the number of persons received on profession of faith or believer's baptism should exceed losses by death by a three-to-one ratio.

F. What Are the Sources of Our New Members?

A reasonable but modest goal for most congregations is for every 100 resident members on the roll, we will receive nine or ten new members annually. Typically six to eight are required to replace losses and the other two or three or four represent a net gain. In the typical American Protestant congregation, three or four of those ten will be received by confession of faith or believer's bap-

O LORD, PLEASE GIVE US A TITHE of PEOPLE for YOUR FAMILY.!!

—FRIAR TUCK,

A reasonable goal is to add ten new members each year for every 100 on our rolls!

tism, four or five will come by letter of transfer from another congregation, and one or two will join by reaffirmation of faith or some similar ritual. This initiatory rite often is used to receive professing Christians who come from a congregation that will not send a letter of transfer.

In the self-identified King-dom-building congregations (see question G in chapter 1), the influx of newcomers is more likely to be in the range of twelve to twenty per 100 members and a substantial majority will join by profession (or reaffirmation) of faith or by believer's baptism.

In the low-expectation churches (see question A of chapter 1) that influx of new-comers is more likely to be in the range of four to seven per 100 resident members and the majority will join by letter of transfer or reaffirmation of faith.

> COME ON IN! THE WATER'S FINE FOREVER!
>
> growing churches that practice "believers' baptism" do so at a ratio of three to four for every 100 members!!
> —FRIAR TUCK

In the congregation-building churches, the influx is more likely to be approximately ten to twelve per 100 resident members and the majority will join by letter of transfer or affirmation.

Five Cautions!

While many will contend this should be number one on any list of statistical self-appraisal questions, it is placed seventh because of inherent limitations. The first and most obvious is the question, what is the definition of membership? This is far from a uniform category! The congregation reporting 1,000 members and 200 as the average worship attendance probably operates with an exceptionally loose and inclusive definition of membership. Dying may not be a

Second, those congregations that include a disproportionately large number of families with children and youth in the nine to fifteen age bracket probably will report a comparatively large number of new members being received by believer's baptism or confession of faith.

Third, those congregations with a very high threshold for membership often report a remarkably high number of new members per 100 full members, but a comparatively low number per 100 average worship attendance.

Fourth, congregations organized within the past two decades normally will receive more new members per 100 resident members than long-established churches.

Finally, churches in communities in which many more people are moving in than are

moving out may have an above average influx of new members, but usually at least one-half of the long-established churches report a modest influx of new members. The usual explanation is they are not competitive with the newer congregations or with older congregations that chose to relocate to a larger site and modern facilities.

TRUST ME, THIS WATER COMES WITH NO SHAMPOO!

— FRIAR TUCK

In growing churches, we need to baptize two babies for every hundred members!

G. How Many Baptisms?

An overlapping question

that suffers from many similar limitations concerns the number of baptisms per 100 resident members. The first limitation is, are we talking about baptisms per 100 resident baptized members or 100 confirmed members? Second, does this congregation practice baptizing people who have been baptized before? Third, what year is it? Are we benefiting from the two big baby booms of 1946–64 and 1987–96? Or the birth dearth era of 1972–78 when the number of births was low? Fourth, does our congregation include many or few families with children at home?

In those congregations that practice infant baptism, a typical ratio is two baptisms annually per 100 resident confirmed members. For those that practice believer's baptism, the ratio is more likely to be close to three or four per 100 resident baptized members.

The crucial question, however, is whether that ratio has been increasing or decreasing.

H. Where Do Our People Live?

Specialized Ministries

"Program, not proximity, determines church participation!"

—FRIAR TUCK

Four underlying trends motivate asking this next self-appraisal question. First, despite the wishes of the advocates of public mass transit, the automobile probably is here to stay. Second, an increasing proportion of teenagers and adults do not build their friendship circles on the basis of the geographical proximity of the place of residence. Third, the journey to work is getting longer as are the journeys to retail stores, to places of recreation, to places for the delivery of health care services, and to the places of worship. Fourth, the younger the constituency of a congregation and/or the more rapid the rate of numerical growth and/or the larger the congregation, the more likely at least one-half of the regular participants live three or more miles away from that congregation's meeting place.

One answer to this question is to place colored pins on a map. Red pins may be used to identify the place of residence of all leaders and teachers. Blue pins may be used to identify the place of residence of all other members who joined at least two years earlier. Green pins may be used for those who have joined during the past two years. What does that distribution of pins tell us? For larger congregations located in communities with postal zip codes that cover a relatively small piece of land, a simpler method is to compare three tables. The first reports the number of people in each zip code who attended worship at least once during that four-Sunday period when the survey of worship attendance was conducted. The second table represents the place of residence, by zip code, of all members who joined more than two years earlier. The third records the number of new members joining during the past two years from each of several zip code areas. These tables can be compared with a similar set of tables prepared ten years earlier. How has the distribution pattern changed?

I. What Is the Age Distribution of Our Members?

Does the age mix of our membership reflect the age distribution of the population? A common pattern is that in congregations founded within the past two decades, the median age for the members will be lower than for the general population in that community. A second pattern is that long-established churches tend to have an older than average group of members. The big exception to this second generalization is many of the congregations that relocated to a new meeting place a few years ago to begin a new era in their history often include many younger new members. A third generalization is that the median age of the American population has been rising since 1970. In 1960 the median age of the American population, thanks to the birth dearth of the 1925–40 era, was 29.5 years. By 1970, thanks to the baby boom of 1946–64, it was down to twenty-eight years. By 1980 it had climbed back up to thirty years and by 1990, thanks to the birth

WELL... THERE GOES THE NEIGHBORHOOD!

AWESOME! I LOVE YOU, MAN! YES!

Growing churches tend to have a younger population than their surrounding communities!!
—FRIAR TUCK

dearth of the mid-1970s and to the miracles of modern medicine, the median age of the American population had jumped to 32.8. In mid-1996, it was 34.3 years and climbing.

Age Distribution American Population
1996

Age	Percent
Birth to 4 years	7.7
5-9	7.3
10-14	7.2
15-19	6.6
20-24	6.9
25-29	7.3
30-34	8.4
35-39	8.6
40-44	7.7
45-49	6.5

Age	*Percent*
50-54	5.1
55-59	4.2
60-64	3.8
65-74	7.1
75+	5.6

Median age 34.3 years.

In many religious traditions young people are not received into full or confirmed membership until age thirteen or fourteen. Therefore in these traditions it will be more useful to compare the congregational age distribution with the population of the United States age fourteen and over. The accompanying table gives that distribution in the United States for 1996.

Age Distribution American Population (1996)

Age	*Percent*
14-17	7.4
18-24	12.3
25-34	18.8
35-44	20.5
45-54	14.8
55-64	10.1
65+	16.1

Median age 40 years.

J. What Is the Marital and Family Distribution?

The past four decades have brought radical changes in the lifestyles of the American population. One is that fewer adults marry. (In 1890, 55 percent of all American women, age fourteen and over, were married. In 1957, that proportion had climbed to 67 percent, and it peaked at 71 percent in 1965. By 1996 it was down to 52 percent.)

Another recent trend is those who do marry tend to marry later in life. A third is families are smaller. A fourth is one-half of all marriages that were terminated last year were ended by divorce rather than by the death of a spouse. A fifth is the increase in the number of one-parent households including children under age eighteen. The first table here reports the living arrangements for Americans, age fifteen and over, in 1996. How does your membership compare with this distribution?

Table I: Living Arrangements

Living alone	12%
Living with spouse	54%
Living with other relatives	27%
Living with nonrelatives	7%

This next table reports the marital status of the American population, age eighteen and over, in 1995.

Table II: Marital Status

Never married	23%
Married	61%
Widowed men	1%

Widowed women	6%
Currently divorced men	4%
Currently divorced women	5%

This third table reports on the distribution of the American population by households in 1995.

Table III: American Households

Married couples without children under 18 at home	29%
Married couples with children under 18 at home	26%
Single mother with children under 18 at home	8%
Single woman without children under 18 at home	5%
Single father with own children under 18 at home	2%
Single man without own children under 18 at home	3%
Man living alone in one-person household	11%
Woman living alone in one-person household	15%

This statistical portrait is slightly more complicated than it appears here since it does not identify that growing proportion of households headed by one or two grandparents and the estimated 14 million young adults, age eighteen to thirty-four who are living with their parents.

The most useful local database may be to develop a consistent set of categories and measure the trend in your congregation over five or ten years. Is the proportion of households with young children increasing or decreasing? Is the proportion of widows increasing or decreasing? What is the trend with adults who live alone?

K. When Was This Congregation Founded?

While there are many exceptions to this generalization, a common pattern for new missions is to reduce their evangelistic outreach by about year seven of their existence as they become increasingly member-oriented. By year twenty or twenty-five, most congregations make taking care of the present members the top priority. Typically three-fourths of all congregations that have been in existence for a quarter of a century or longer are experiencing a decline in worship attendance or are on a plateau in size.

One BIG exception to this common pattern of institutional behavior is the long-established congregation that several years ago decided the time had come to reach a new constituency and relocated the meeting place as one component of that larger strategy. The key decision was not the relocation of the meeting place and the construction of new facilities. A common scenario placed first that decision to identify and reach a new or a larger constituency. That was followed by preparation of a ministry plan that recognized and included the need for better physical facilities, more meeting rooms, a much larger narthex, a huge increase in off-street parking, better space for worship, and a modern nursery. Sometimes this led to the initial decision to remodel and build at that historic site, but after everyone had time for second thoughts, it was decided to make a fresh start for a new era of that congregation's history at a new location. While the congregation may be able to trace its history back to 1882 or 1923 or 1954 or 1975, it now resembles a rapidly growing seven-year-old new mission.

Has the time come for your eighty or 100-year-old congregation to make a fresh start at a new location?

(The second BIG exception are the self-identified Kingdom-building congregations described in the previous chapter.)

Less common, but growing rapidly in numbers is the congregation founded several decades earlier that discusses the question, has the time come to relocate our meeting place in order to serve a new constituency or should we stay here? The response is an enthusiastic, Yes!

These congregations continue their ministry from what to them has become an historic site, but rent, lease, or purchase one or more additional sites in order to reach people who cannot or will not come to that traditional meeting place.

One multisite congregation built a new set of buildings on a thirty-acre site to reach and serve families moving into a new residential area while continuing a full scale ministry out of that historic downtown building. Another launches three-to-five off-campus ministries annually to reach precisely and narrowly defined new constituencies. Many of these multisite congregations are self-identified Kingdom-building churches.

When was your congregation founded? When did you complete the last major construction program at this site? Has the time arrived to look at another site to enable you to reach new constituencies? Should the generation of members who joined since completion of the last major construction program be challenged to reach new constituencies? Has the time come to evolve into a multisite congregation?

CHAPTER THREE

What Is Our Purpose? What Is Our Community Image?

The most widely followed, the most difficult, frequently the most divisive, often the least useful, and sometimes the most time consuming beginning point for the deliberations of a long-range planning committee is to agree on a statement of purpose. One solution is a broad and inclusive statement worded in the appropriately pious language that cannot offend anyone—and provides limited direction. Frequently it is far too long for leaders to be able to memorize.

The big benefit is the process may force the members to engage in extensive, serious, and revealing discussions about the nature of the New Testament church and how those images can provide direction for contemporary planning.

Another common beginning point is for the members to seek to agree on a more narrowly defined vision of what they believe God is calling that particular congregation to be and to be doing in the immediate future.

A. What Is the Operational Statement of Purpose?

If, however, the first assignment for this committee is congregational self-appraisal, a useful approach to this task of defin-

ing purpose may be to ask this question. If a complete stranger came and identified everything we do under the label of what we call ministry, what would that stranger conclude is the operational definition of our purpose? In other words, let us define our current purpose by what we do, not by what we say.

In thousands of today's congregations, that stranger might come up with an operational statement of purpose resembling this. On the basis of what was seen and heard, it appears this congregation operates with this twelve point statement of purpose:

1. Provide loving pastoral care of the members, and especially the long-tenured older members, by a minister who genuinely loves people.
2. Encourage as many members as possible to gather once or twice a week for corporate worship.
3. Build a caring community of believers who will be a mutual support base for one another.

4. Offer weekly sermons and adult classes designed to help believers become better Christians and to help them become better informed about our doctrines and our belief system.

5. Seek to transmit the Christian faith to younger generations.

6. Collect and send away a respectable sum of money to finance the work of other people engaged in Christian ministry in other places.

7. Maintain our real estate, which for many of us has become a sacred place.

8. Provide the context of a worshiping community for such religious experiences as baptism, the Lord's Supper, marriages, and memorial services following the death of a loved one.

9. Take reasonably good care of our pastor.

10. Within the limitations of our resources, do good in this community.

11. Provide as many meaningful small face-to-face group experiences for our people as are deemed necessary.

12. Collect the money required to pay for all of the above.

The next question for that self-appraisal committee could be this. Are we satisfied with that statement of purpose? If that does represent contemporary reality, are there changes that should be made? Should we change the

LISTEN...
UNLESS YOU TWO
GET ON BOARD
WE WON'T SAIL!

Do our operational goals reinforce a sense of community?
—FRIAR TUCK

rank order? Should we add to that list? Should we redefine any of those twelve points?

B. Are We Happy with That Operational Statement?

In one twenty-year-old congregation, the self-appraisal committee made these changes in a similar operational statement of purpose.

1. We must place persuading nonbelievers to become believers as our first reason for existing.
2. We cannot be content simply with seeking to make our members into better Christians, we must seek to transform believers into disciples of Jesus Christ.
3. Instead of seeking only to transmit the Christian faith to our youth, we must concentrate on discipling our teenagers.
4. In addition to sending money away to finance the ministries of others, we should challenge, motivate, enlist, train, nurture, place, and support volunteers from our congregation who will be engaged in doing ministry beyond the boundaries of our congregation.

5. In addition to helping our members become better informed about the Christian faith, we must enable them to increase their capability to articulate their faith.
6. As we seek to reach a larger

and more diversified constituency, we must offer at least two or three choices in what can be meaningful worship experiences.

7. We must expand the range of opportunities for people, including nonmembers, to be involved in meaningful small face-to-face groups.

8. Instead of focusing on raising the money required to pay our bills, we should concentrate on encouraging our members to become better stewards of all that has been entrusted to them by God.

Taking good care of the pastor, perpetuating the past into tomorrow, and underwriting the budget did not make this revised and shorter operational statement of purpose.

If this is a new mission, it may be wise to gather together several prospective charter members to formulate a statement of purpose.

If, however, this is a long-established congregation, it may be more useful to begin by defining the operational statement of purpose.

C. How Do Others See Us?

A parallel step in this self-appraisal process is to ask two more questions. First, what is the image of this congregation that we project to others? How do nonmembers in this com-

How does your community perceive your church?
— FRIAR TUCK

munity see us? What is our community image? When residents discuss the churches in this community, what do they say about us?

The answer may begin with these words, "That church is best known for ..." and then they complete that sentence. For example, someone might comment, "That church is known for its emphasis on missions. They give fifty cents out of every dollar to missions and dozens of their members have gone to serve in the mission field." Another congregation may be described as, "That church is theologically the most liberal congregations in town." A third might be referred to as, "That church has the best ministry of music of any church around here." Another may be identified, "That church is a blue collar congregation." A small, but growing number are identified as, "That is the church that specializes in saving troubled marriages. My neighbor says her marriage would have ended in divorce if it hadn't been for the help of a mentoring couple from that congregation."[1]

In other places that sentence might be completed with statements such as these: "... its excellent Christian day school" or "... for being a truly multicultural fellowship," or "... its day camp for children that operates five days a week all summer" or "... reaching large numbers of young couples in their twenties" or "... the largest singles' ministry in the county" or "... offering both English and Spanish language worship every Sunday morning" or "... openly and unre-

servedly welcoming gays and lesbians into full membership"
or "... relying entirely on lay volunteers, rather than paid
ministers, to preach and lead worship every Sunday" or "...
specializing in ministry with couples in interfaith marriages"
or "... its off-campus ministries" or "... being the number
one choice for students in the local college or university" or
"... having ten to fifteen worshipers in wheelchairs every
Sunday" or "... operating a soup kitchen seven days a week"
or "... welcoming self-identified charismatic Christians" or
"... their summer school for gifted children for two weeks
every June" or "... their job training program for the unem-
ployed" or "... that medical clinic in the church building" or
"... their Saturday evening worship service designed by and
for young adults in the eighteen to twenty-five age bracket"
or "... housing an extension center of a theological seminary" or "... their large number of active and recently
retired farmers" or "... honoring all the educators in this
community at their Sunday morning worship service on
Labor Day Sunday every year" or "... being the only pre-
dominantly white congregation in town with a black pastor"
or "... the oldest church building in this community" or "...
providing a shelter for the homeless every Wednesday night
of the year" or "... reporting a larger Sunday school attendance than worship attendance" or "... offering a ministry
with parents and their babies" or "... their German language
worship service every Sunday morning" or "... feeding more
than a thousand people and raising over $5,000 for missions
with their big barbeque the second Saturday in August every
year" or "... their prekindergarten nursery school for children ages two through five years" or "... having a former
Roman Catholic priest as their pastor" or "... their full array
of Sunday school classes for developmentally disabled children" or "... their pastor who also is the number one community leader among all the clergy here" or "... housing the
weekly meeting of more than a dozen mutual support

groups" or "... the smallest worship attendance of any church in town" or "... the largest high school youth group in town" or "... their full and complete commitment to ecumenism on the local level" or "... frequently initiating new cooperative interchurch ministries designed to serve the larger community" or "... attracting well over 1,800 people to the two Easter Sunday services they hold in the civic auditorium every year" or "... bringing in nationally known preachers for their Wednesday evening Lenten services every year" or "... running six different weeks of vacation Bible school every summer" or "... pulling off a highly successful relocation effort " or "... scheduling seven different services on Christmas Eve" or "... dismissing each of their last three pastors" or "... hosting the weekly meetings of the Lions Club" or "... being the local base for Young Life ministries" or "... their strong public pro-life stance" or "... their ultraconservative theological stance" or "... their ministries with senior citizens" or "... their efforts to resettle refugees from Southeast Asia."

What is the community image outsiders carry of your congregation?

D. Are You Happy with That Image?

The last question is very simple. Are you happy with the image outsiders have of your congregation? If not, what is the image you want them to carry in their heads? How can you make that happen?

The central thesis of this chapter is easy to articulate. Instead of beginning with a blank sheet of paper to articulate your mission statement or your definition of purpose in a self-appraisal process, it may be more useful to begin by defining contemporary reality. How far is that definition removed from your vision of the ideal world? How do you get from here to there?

When embarking on a journey, it is helpful to know the destination. It is even more crucial, however, to know the place of departure. The passage of time may change the destination, but the starting point is fixed.

The same is true when appraising the image of this congregation held by outsiders. The definition of contemporary reality can be a useful beginning point. The responses to the questions in the first two chapters can inform this definition of contemporary reality.

CHAPTER FOUR

Who Will Be Tomorrow's New Members?

WHEN DOES A CHURCH BECOME A HAUNTED HOUSE?

—FRIAR TUCK

When those who want to grow old together scare away young people!

Another set of congregational self-appraisal questions begins with a simple statement of fact. Sooner or later all the present members of your congregation will do one of three things. They will (1) drop out, or (2) move away, or (3) die. Some will do all three. This leaves your leaders with three alternatives, (1) go out of business after the next-to-last funeral, or (2) assume this will not reach a crisis stage until we are gone and so we will let the next generation of leaders worry about that, or (3) evaluate the present system of enlisting future constituencies to determine where improvements should be made.

The best congregations will not be motivated by

institutional survival, but rather by Matthew 28:19-20. In either approach, these eight self-appraisal questions can be useful beginning points.

A. How Long Is the List of Prospective Future Members?

In congregations where the threshold for becoming a member is very high and the average worship attendance is at least double the number of resident full members, that list should be at least the length of the membership list.

In midlevel-expectation congregations where the worship attendance-to-membership is between 60 and 90 percent, the list should be at least one-half the membership list.

In low-commitment congregations in which the attendance-to-membership ratio is below 40 percent, a reasonable goal is the number of prospective new members will be equal to one-sixth to one-half the number of resident full members.

B. Who Is Responsible for That List?

Does anyone maintain the list of prospective new members, building relationships with the people who appear on it? If the answer is "no," skip the rest of this chapter and move on to the questions in the next chapter.

C. How Many First-Time Visitors Worship with Us Each Weekend?

If the answer is a number smaller than 2 percent of the total worship attendance, ask why. Is the number one entry point for that first contact with potential future members other than Sunday worship? This could be adult Bible study

HMM-M, I'M AT CHURCH, IT MUST BE TUESDAY NIGHT!

— FRIAR TUCK

Weekday programming is now the #1 entry point for young adults into a congregation !

classes or mutual support groups or Christmas Eve or Labor Day Sunday or parenting classes or special events or a Christian day school or a recreation program or social justice ministries or vacation Bible school or trips or ministries with families with teenagers or specialized ministries with women or community outreach ministries or door-to-door visitation or television or a sidewalk Sunday school or a weekday preschool ministry or a pastoral counseling center.

If your congregation reports relatively few first-time visitors at worship and if it does not offer an extensive weekday program, you probably have limited appeal to prospective future members.

If the goal is to focus on nonbelievers and/or unchurched believers, rather than on people who have a current or very recent active church relationship, weekday and weeknight (including Saturday night) ministries often are more effective initial points of contact than is Sunday morning worship.

D. How Many New Face-to-Face Groups?[1]

If the goal is to both reach and assimilate future new members, a healthy response is that the congregation organized two of such groups with seven to thirty-five participants for each 100 to 150 persons in average worship attendance. The directing slogan is "New groups for new people."

E. How Many New Full Members Did We Receive Last Year?

This question should be exclusive of children under age fifteen. Those congregations with a high threshold for membership, in which worship attendance exceeds membership, often report only five to ten new members annually per 100 full members. Their big increase in numbers is in constituents.

Social networks catch the lonely before they become the lost!

The midlevel-expectation churches with a lower threshold for membership plus a strong and well-organized evangelistic system are more likely to report eight to fifteen new members per 100 resident full members. (The reason for excluding new members age fifteen and under is that this figure is largely a reflection of the age and marital status of today's members rather than of a capability to reach the unchurched.)

F. Has That Ratio of New Members Received to Resident Full Members Been Going Up or Down During the Past Several Years?

Here again the two crucial questions are, What is the trend line and why is that the recent trend.

G. What Are the Ages and Marital Characteristics of Our New Members?

A comparison of the age and marital status of the adults who have joined the congregation in the last two years with the total membership (see questions I and J in chapter 2) will suggest whether or not this congregation is following the homogeneous unit principle ("birds of a feather flock together" or churches tend to attract people who resemble the current membership), or is reaching a broader slice of the chur :hgoing market, or is reaching a new constituency.

H. Can We Interview Our Past Visitors?

The most revealing, and also the most difficult of these eight questions requires building a list of all first-time visitors at worship. That list should be divided into three parts. The part that will be the most satisfying consists of those first-time visitors who re-turned and eventually united with this congregation as full members. Ask each one five questions:

Religious Pilgrimages

HOPE

I don't see it as church-hopping but as visits among god's many mansions!

—FRIAR TUCK

1. What motivated you to come that first time?
2. What motivated you to return?
3. What motivated you to join?
4. What do you believe we as a congregation do best?
5. What can we do to improve our relationship with visitors who are potential future members?

The second, and sometimes longer section of that larger list, includes the visitors who have returned to worship here on at least three or more occasions, but have not united with this congregation. Ask each one these six questions:

WHEW! *from* WHENCE TO WHEREVER...

People on a religious pilgrimage are as unpredictable as the wind!
—FRIAR TUCK

1. What motivated you to worship here on that first occasion? When?
2. What motivated you to return? How often?
3. Are you interested in becoming a member of this congregation?
4. If not, what is the reason?
5. Are you also concurrently worshiping with another congregation? Who? Why?
6. What could we do to make this congregation more responsive to your needs?

At this point in the discussion a question must be raised about the definition of the "unchurched" population in your community. Typically a somewhat oversimplified definition of that term includes five categories of people without a current and active relationship to any church in your community. A highly visible group consists of self-identified believers who are actively searching for a new church home. In many congregations these account for most of the first-time visitors.

A second category consists of self-identified Christians who, for one reason or another, are not involved in the life

of any worshiping community and are not actively searching for a church home. In many communities this is the largest of these five groups.

The third group consists of the self-identified nonbelievers, the atheists, and the agnostics.

A fourth group includes children and youth who have not yet made a public declaration of their faith in Jesus Christ as Lord and Savior. In many congregations, confirmation classes represent the primary effort to reach this segment of the population and the focus is largely on children of members. In other churches, the ministries with families that include teenagers is the number one channel for reaching this slice of the population. In some churches the primary focus in the youth program is on children of members while in other congregations one-fourth to one-half of the families involved do not have any current active relationship.

The fifth group is increasing in numbers in the larger metropolitan areas and includes members of non-Christian religious bodies.

Which of these five groups account for most of your recent new members? Which of the five is the top priority in your evangelistic outreach? Is that intentional?

The third section frequently is the longest of the three parts of this list. In those congregations with a high-quality ministry that is designed to be relevant to the needs of people at several different stages of one's religious pilgrimage, as many as 80 percent of the resident first-time visitors settle in to become regular worshipers, some as members, others as nonmember constituents. In most North American Protestant congregations, however, fewer than one-half of the first-time visitors who do not have kinfolk or very close friends among the members, eventually become members.

This third section includes the names of those first-time visitors who never returned or came back only once or twice before disappearing completely. In arranging an appointment with these former visitors, it may be helpful to preface it with this request. "We are in the process of a serious self-appraisal of the life and ministry of Thusands Church. We could benefit by your help if you would be willing to give us twenty to thirty minutes of your time for someone to come and talk with you. If that is not possible, perhaps you could

IF WE'RE NOT AFRAID *of* BAD NEWS ... GULP!

Those who go elsewhere can be a valuable asset in evaluating a church's ministries!
—FRIAR TUCK

respond to our questions over the telephone. When would be a convenient time for someone to come and call on you? Or would you prefer we do this by telephone?" (Offer the choice of personal visit or telephone, not the choice of "yes," or "no, thanks.")

Our records indicate that you worshiped with us at least once during the past year.

1. What motivated you to come and worship with our congregation?
2. What was the reception you experienced on that first visit?
3. Have you worshiped with us since that first time?
4. Have you found a church home yet? If so, what is the name?
5. What could we have done to be more effective in responding to your needs?
6. Do you have any advice you could give to our leaders on how we could be more effective as a church?

The big advantage of the face-to-face personal interview is that usually provides a better setting to ask relevant and specific follow-up questions evoked by the responses to these more general inquiries.

A common fringe benefit of the personal visits is 5 to 10 percent of those visited conclude, "Maybe your church is the place for me after all."

If the eight questions raised in this chapter are combined with the responses to questions A, C, D, E, and F in the first chapter plus the responses to all eleven of the questions in the second chapter plus the responses evoked by the second and fourth questions in this previous chapter, this information should enable the self-appraisal committee to suggest what needs to be done if this congregation expects to reach and serve new generations of people in the decades ahead.

CHAPTER FIVE

How Are We Organized?

While one could argue that this is really a means-to-an-end question that belongs in chapter 6, from the perspective of the long-range planning committee this is a critical policy question. It can be stated in more precise terms with six questions.

A. Permission-Giving or Permission-Withholding?

How do members of the governing board see their role? Is the basic assumption that permission will be withheld unless a persuasive argument can be made on behalf of a new ministry, a change in the schedule, a new program, a new approach to worship, a new style of youth ministries, and other proposed changes? Or do the members of the

DON'T EVEN THINK IT!

GULP!

—FRIAR TUCK©

Some governing boards believe their major role is to veto every goal!

governing board begin with the assumption that they are a permission-granting body unless persuasive arguments can be offered against a proposed change?

Are we organized to perpetuate the status quo, or to be open to innovation and new ideas?

Do committees and task forces perceive the governing board to be a barrier to be overcome, or as an ally creating a new tomorrow?

Will that governing board look favorably on the recommendations for changes that come out of the deliberations of this long-range planning committee? Will we have to develop a strategy to overcome their probable opposition, or can we enlist them as allies in this continuing process?

B. Abundance or Scarcity?

Are decisions made on the assumption that there is a potential abundance of resources or a scarcity? This can be illustrated by contrasting two sets of responses to new ideas.

"Why should we add a second worship service to the Sunday morning schedule when half of the pews are now empty at the one service?"

"We are convinced that if we can attract more people, we can arrange the schedule to provide the room to accommodate them."

"That may be a good idea, and I can see the need for that new ministry, but where can we find the volunteers to staff it?"

"We act on the assumption that if the need is real and if we are effective in explaining that need to our members, we can enlist as many volunteers as we need to staff that new ministry."

"We prepare the expenditure half of our budget for the coming year after we have added up the pledges we have received from our people.

"We prepare our budget of proposed expenditures for the coming year in response to what we see as the needs we are called to address. The Stewardship Committee, which is completely unrelated to our Budget Committee, challenges people to give in response to how the Lord has blessed them."

The larger the church the smaller the influence of its governing board!

—FRIAR TUCK

What are your priorities for off-street parking!

— FRIAR TUCK

C. Care of Members or Welcome to Strangers?

Is your weekend schedule designed in response to the wishes of your members, or to attract more first-time visitors?

What are the priorities for your off-street parking arrangements? To encourage people to come early? To reward early arrivals? To make mothers of young children feel they are expected and welcomed? To make first-time visitors feel welcome? To welcome the disabled? To guarantee paid staff members a reserved parking space? To convey a feeling of safety to women coming alone after dark?

Who determines the type of music used in worship? The pastor? The choir director? The choir? The board? The preferences of long-time members? Previous generations? The evangelism committee? An ad hoc task force of worshipers born after 1969? Is the number one goal of the ministry of music to praise and please

God? To welcome and assimilate newcomers? To please the current membership?

How difficult is it for a first-time visitor to follow and participate in worship at your church? How easy is it for a complete stranger (a) to find the correct door to enter during the week, (b) to discover where we worship, (c) to come to an adult class, and (d) to come to a special weeknight meeting held in this building?

Are we bound by local traditions or sensitive to the needs of today?
—FRIAR TUCK

Are the sermons designed on the assumption that everyone in the room is a Christian and a member of this congregation? To persuade skeptics, searchers, seekers, agnostics, and others on a religious quest of the truth and relevance of the Christian gospel? To challenge believers to become disciples? To help believers become better Christians?

If Holy Communion is a part of every worship service on every weekend, when and how do you welcome nonbelievers, skeptics, inquirers, seekers, searchers, and others on a self-identified religious quest?

D. What Is the Crucial Dividing Line Between the Laity and the Paid Staff?

Is your church organized on the assumption that the clergy will do the ministry and the laity will (a) attend, (b) pay the bills, (c) staff administrative boards and committees,

GULP! I'M SURROUNDED
BY EVERYONE BUT FRIENDS!

Allies are essential
to any action plan!

—FRIAR TUCK

(d) teach in the Sunday school, and (e) staff the gender and age-defined organizations (women's organization, men's fellowship, youth program)?

Or is your church organized on the assumption that the laity will make the hospital calls, teach, lead worship, evangelize, staff outreach ministries, and suggest the creation of new ministries while the paid staff will (a) preach, (b) administer the sacraments, (c) administer the institution, and (d) chal-lenge, motivate, enlist, train, nurture, and support lay volunteers in doing most of the ministry?

E. What Is Our Self-Image?

How do we conceptualize our church? As a congregation of two hundred members or of ninety families? A congregation of two crowds—those who come to the early worship service and those who worship at the later hour? As the church at the corner of X and Y Boulevard? As the only franchise of our denomination in this community? As a place that provides employment for a dozen adults? As a network of small groups? As a precisely defined nationality, language, or ethnic congregation? As a warm and friendly fellowship? As a congregation of classes, circles, cells, choirs, services, organizations, and fellowships? Or as Pastor So-and-so's church?

How does that answer impact your organizational structure?

F. What Is the Stance of Our Pastor?

This often is the number one question in any self-appraisal process. While most pastors are not able single-handedly to initiate and implement substantial changes, any pastor who ranks above the bottom 10 percent in competence can veto any change that someone else proposes.

The existence of a self-appraisal or special planning committee, even if initiated by someone else, usually is evidence that the pastor is at least open to new ideas and change. The wise pastor who displays a strong affection for the status quo and/or opposes any increase in his or her workload and/or feels threatened by change usually can either (a) veto the creation of any self-appraisal or planning effort or (b) undermine it if that veto is overridden. This introduces the first question to be asked in this stage of the self-appraisal process.

What is the position of the current pastor on the status quo versus change? In one congregation, for example, the pastor made it clear, "I plan to retire in three years, and no one is going to rock this boat until after I leave!"

Second, is your pastor more comfortable (a) with a small church style of ministry[1] or (b) with a large church style of ministry?[2]

Third, does your pastor prefer (a) to do the ministry (lead worship, teach, make

If I had any higher expectations of our members they might drop me (GULP!)!

FRIAR TUCK

How much space will we need by the year 2025?

"...most new ideas are rejected the first time or two they are presented!"

hospital calls, evangelize, preach, initiate new classes, and so forth) or (b) to enlist, motivate, challenge, train, nurture, and support volunteers who will do much of the ministry?

Fourth, does the pastor place the top priority on (a) taking better care of today's members or (b) designing and implementing a strategy to reach the unchurched?

Fifth, does the pastor (a) act on the assumption that tomorrow will be a carbon copy of yesterday or (b) look forward eagerly to the challenges a new day will bring?

Sixth, what is the position of the pastor on the theological spectrum? If the pastor is to the right of most of the members, there is a fifty-fifty probability that the church will be a numerically growing congregation. If the pastor is to the left of most of the members, the chances are three out of four this will be a numerically shrinking congregation.

Finally, does the current pastor expect (a) to be the pastor of this congregation ten years from now or (b) to move within the next several years?

In summary, is this congregation organized to encourage creativity, innovation, and new ideas? Or is it organized to perpetuate yesterday as long as possible?

CHAPTER SIX

Means-to-an-End Questions

These four questions are placed near the end of the book not because they are unimportant, but for two other reasons. The first is that too often these are the first questions raised in the congregational self-appraisal process. Thus they can become diversionary issues that distract from that more crucial discussion of purpose, role, and contemporary reality.

Second, they are placed late in this book because most of them raise issues that cannot be discussed in a meaningful manner except in the context of the responses to earlier questions. This can be illustrated by four common patterns of institutional behavior among the churches.

First, how large is the paid program staff? Frequently a relatively large proportion of total expenditures are allocated to the compensation of paid staff in (a) low-expectation congregations, (b) congregations experiencing numerical decline, (c) churches with a comparatively low ratio of worship attendance-to-membership, (d) congregations without a clearly defined role or constituency, (e) congregations in which the median age of the confirmed (age fourteen and over) membership is past fifty, (f) congregations that include a large proportion of older one-person households, (g) congregations that place a high priority on ordained staff who are full-time generalists rather than on part-time lay specialists, (h) congregations that are affiliated with a religious heritage organized around a distrust of the laity,[1] (i) congregations in which the median tenure of the current membership is twelve years or more, and (j) churches in which many of the members of the governing board believe a major role for the board is to tell other people what they cannot do.

When a congregation displays three or four of these characteristics, it often has a larger paid staff than is the norm.

Second, how much land is required for the meeting place? For the downtown church in a large city, it may be 20,000 square feet of land or less (one-half acre) per 1,000 average worship attendance. At the other end of this spectrum is the relatively new (or relocated) regional church that houses on the campus a worshiping community averaging 2,500 at weekend worship, an extensive ministry with parents of very young children, a large drama group, a Christian school K–12, a theological seminary, a retirement community, a huge ministry of recreation, a retreat center with an emphasis on lay training, an exceptionally large seven-day-a-week ministry, and residential facilities for children from severely dysfunctional families. That site may average out to over 2 million square feet (fifty acres) of land per 1,000 people at worship.

Third, what is the level of member contributions? The most obvious variable is that *per member* average probably will be much higher in the 200 member congregation that has a very high threshold for membership and averages 800 at worship, than it will be in the 800 member church that averages 200 at worship.

Fourth, the weekend schedule of the congregation primarily designed to serve people who have passed their fiftieth birthday probably will be less complicated and offer far fewer choices than the schedule in the same size congregation that is designed to reach and serve people from several generations.

Despite the limitations of these and similar variables, the self-appraisal process should include these four questions.

A. How Much Land Do We Need?

In the ideal world the answer is at least one acre for every 100 people at worship on the weekend. Thus the congregation with an average attendance of seventy-five at the Saturday evening worship, 120 at the early Sunday morning service, 180 at the second Sunday service, and 125 on Monday evening should be comfortable on a five-acre site. The addition of a Christian K–8 elementary school and/or a Christian high school and/or a retirement village and/or a seminary extension center and/or a regional retreat center and/or a weekday child care program and/or an extensive summer day camping ministry and/or a big recreation program obviously will require more land.

What are the alternatives if the congregation owns only two acres of land with no available adjacent property, and that church now averages 500 at worship on Sunday morning?

1. Watch passively and helplessly as the attendance declines over the next few decades.
2. Spread what is now concentrated in Sunday morning out over the week.
3. Relocate to a larger site.
4. Build a powerful political lobby that will drastically increase the costs of the ownership and use of privately owned motor vehicles and make public mass transit the primary vehicle for moving people.
5. Expand the physical facilities to four or five stories.

6. Acquire additional meeting places and become a multi-site congregation.[2]
7. Begin earlier with breakfast at 7 A.M. on Sunday morning and schedule three or four different worship experiences between 8 A.M. and 3 P.M.

Another alternative is to gather together a group of long-tenured members who will recall how "we accommodated many more people in this amount of space back in 1950" and ask, "If we did it then, why can't we do it today?" The answer, of course, is many of those adults of 1950 are now dead and are not the pillars on which to re-create 1950.

A better alternative is to attempt to project the amount of space that will be required by this congregation in 2025, which is much closer in time than is 1950, and begin to design a ministry plan to meet those projected needs.

B. How Much Money Do We Need?

The beginning point in 1998 for this discussion is $1,000 annually times the annual average worship attendance or, approximately, twenty dollars per week per worshiper.

That figure may be only ten to fifteen dollars per week per worshiper in the small rural church served by a bivocational pastor or a bivocational team. It may be closer to forty dollars per worshiper per week in the rapidly growing congregation where nine dollars of those forty are allocated for benevolences, missions, and denominational causes and another ten dollars are allocated to a building fund and/or debt retirement. That figure may be closer to forty-five dollars per week in that large congregation with a low threshold of membership that encourages checkbook participation, allocates seven or eight of those forty-five dollars to benevolences, missions, and denominational causes, is served by a busy staff committed to doing ministry (rather than enlisting and training volunteers), and in which personality and credentials are given more weight than performance in determining staff compensation.

If the goal is to allocate the first fifty cents out of every dollar to benevolences, it probably will be necessary to receive at least thirty-five to fifty dollars per worshiper per week to be able to meet that goal and also carry on a full scale seven-day-a-week ministry. Expenditures for capital needs must be added to that figure of thirty-five to fifty dollars per worshiper per week.

At this point someone on the self-appraisal task force should raise this question, "Is our top priority to raise money to send away to hire someone else to do ministry on our behalf? Or is our top priority to challenge, motivate, enlist, train, nurture, and support our people who will be engaged in doing ministry in various places?" Is the emphasis on asking members to "pray and pay" for missions or to do ministry?

A simple example of this distinction is, Does this congregation plant one new mission every few years or does it send money away to hire someone else to organize new congregations?

An internal example of this is the difference between hiring a youth pastor to work directly with teenagers and finding a staff person who will build and train a cadre of volunteers to work with families that include teenagers.

The parallel is the difference between the staff person who works with the missions committee to decide which benevolent causes to support financially and the minister of missions who works with a missions council to create and staff with volunteers a network of off-campus ministries.[3]

Finally, these figures must be adjusted upward in high-cost communities and they can be adjusted downward in low-cost communities.

At this point someone is likely to interrupt and ask, "Where will we get all that money? If you can go to the movies for three or five or six dollars, why would anyone give twenty or thirty dollars to come to church?"

The obvious answer is that since you don't sell popcorn, you have to charge more.

A better answer is that with one big exception, you probably will not receive all your required funds from one source. That big exception is the congregation in which (a) tithing has been a way of life for at least a couple of decades and (b) nearly all of everyone's tithe is returned to the Lord through that congregation's treasury.

Today an increasing number of congregations depend on ten to fifteen of the following income streams to finance the ministry and outreach of that church.

1. *The Offering Plate.* This is the only one that is close to universal. Nearly all congregations pass the offer-

LET'S SEE...THERE'S USER FEES, AN OFFERING PLATE, PLUS MEMORIALS...

NO EXPRESS LANE

It now takes a variety of income sources to meet a church's weekly needs!
—FRIAR TUCK

ing plates or baskets at every worship service. Typically this is the largest single income stream. It often accounts for somewhere between 50 and 100 percent of the total dollar receipts for the year.

2. *User Fees.* The fastest growing income stream consists of fees charged the consumers of services. These include tuition for a weekday preschool program, charges for child care, fees for vacation Bible school, and fees for special programs, trips, events, meals, evening classes, and other programs.

3. *Memorials.* For a growing number of congregations, memorial gifts are used to pay for a variety of needs ranging from new hymnals to renovation of the parlor to a new van to air conditioning. It is not unusual for memorial gifts to constitute 5 to 10 percent of total annual receipts.

4. *Bequests.* Between 1980 and 2020 the generations born before 1935 will

give away more than $8 trillion. Part of that will be in the form of bequests to churches. The bequest of $100,000 to $500,000 is not uncommon today. Perhaps one-tenth of the very large bequests come from nonmembers. A growing number of congregations actively encourage their members to remember that church in their wills.

5. *Large Gifts.* The current tax code encourages wealthy individuals to make generous, one-time gifts to charitable organizations.

6. *Income from Investments.* The combination of bequests and large individual gifts has created a growing number of congregations with their own endowment fund or foundation. This can produce a steady income stream from those investments. This may amount to 10 to 40 percent of all receipts.

7. *Sales.* Many congregations receive gifts of real estate or personal property. Others sell off surplus real estate. A rapidly growing number operate a bookstore and/or cafeteria on campus. For these churches, sales may be a substantial income stream in a particular year.

8. *The Small Appeal.* Sometimes referred to as nickel and dime askings, thousands of churches schedule from five to seventy modest special appeals annually. Typically each one yields an amount equal to one to five dollars times the attendance at that particular worship service.

9. *The BIG Appeal.* Sometimes referred to as Miracle Sunday, a growing number of congregations are choosing one weekend to raise a large sum of money. Usually this is equal to one-third to three times last year's total receipts from member contributions. While the money placed in the offering plate week after week usually comes from the current income of the contributor, this appeal is based on the assumption people will give out of their accumulated wealth or savings.[4]

10. *The Three-Year Capital Funds Appeal.* This income stream usually is reserved for either (a) capital expenditures or (b) mortgage reduction, but it often accounts for one-fourth to one-half of the total dollar receipts in a particular year.

11. *Rentals.* Many congregations are renting out part of their facilities to a child care organization, an immigrant church, or to a nonprofit agency. It is not uncommon for these rentals to represent one-fifth to one-half of the total receipts for the year in congregations where the top priority is institutional survival.

12. *The Outsider.* When confronted with the need for money to finance (a) expensive capital improvements, (b) reconstruction of the physical plant after a natural

disaster such as a tornado, earthquake, or flood, or (c) a new community ministry such as a health center or a child care program or an adult day care program or a shelter for the homeless, many congregations find it easy to encourage contributions from nonmembers.

13. *Foundations and Corporations.* Thousands of congregations have received large grants from corporations or philanthropic foundations to (a) preserve and restore a historic building, (b) initiate a new community ministry such as feeding the hungry or a latchkey program or staffing a counseling center, or (c) offer extensive summer programs for children.

14. *Governments.* By creating separate 501(c)3 corporations, hundreds of congregations now receive governmental funds for housing rehabilitation or job training or counseling persons with AIDS or ministries with developmentally disabled children or preschool programs and other social welfare ministries. This may become the fastest-growing income stream for churches during the next dozen years. Legislation adopted by the federal government in 1995, 1996, and 1997 has sharply increased the potential size of this income stream for churches.

15. *Money-Raising Events.* This is an old standby that includes dinners, bake sales, plays, bazaars, rummage sales, and auctions. For many small rural churches, this income stream may be the difference between a full-time resident pastor and sharing a minister with another congregation.

16. *Denominational Subsidies.* For literally thousands of congregations from 1960 to 1990, this was the fastest-growing income stream. In recent years, it is being reconsidered because of (a) the shortage of funds in denominational treasuries, and (b) questions being raised about the efficacy of subsidies.

The members of the congregational self-appraisal committee may want to ask themselves these questions.

1. Using this list as a beginning point, what are the potential income streams for this congregation?
2. How many of those potential income streams are now being utilized by this congregation?
3. Is that a satisfactory number? Or do you want to either increase or decrease the number?
4. What are the values that will guide the decision-making process as you make that decision?
5. What steps must be taken to add a new income stream to the financial base of this congregation?
6. Or do you prefer the alternative of creating a high-expectation congregation in which one of the requirements for membership is that every candidate for membership (a) must be a tither

and (b) is expected to return to the Lord via that congregation's treasury at least one-half of that tithe?

7. Another widely used alternative is to reduce proposed
   expenditures to match anticipated receipts.

8. Which alternative will you recommend?

C. How Much Staff Do We Need?

This means-to-an-end
question is by far the most
difficult because of three
critical variables. First, on a
scale of one to six to measure
productivity, most church
staff members are in the
three to four range. The congregation staffed by highly
productive people (those
who score a five and the rare
ones who score a six) obviously needs less than half the
number of people on the
payroll as the congregation
staffed largely by people who score one, two, or three on that
scale.

Perhaps one-half of that difference in productivity levels is
in the gifts, training, work habits, competence, experience,
personality, and skills of the individuals. The other one-half
usually is in the work environment. As a general rule, the
more precisely and clearly defined the responsibilities for a
staff person *and* the more closely they match the gifts, skills,
interests, and experience level of that person, the higher the
level of productivity. For obvious reasons, one being the
learning curve, the best of the long-tenured pastors usually

are more productive workers than the best of the short-tenured pastors.

The second variable, which has been mentioned in earlier chapters, reflects the distinction between hiring staff to do ministry and choosing staff who focus on challenging, motivating, enlisting, training, placing, nurturing, and supporting volunteers. (See question H in chapter 1.)

HER ONLY BLESSED TALENT SEEMS TO BE TO INSPIRE FOLKS FOR MINISTRY!

The best use of a church staff is in challenging, training and supporting volunteers!
— FRIAR TUCK

The third variable also reflects the productivity issue. As a general rule, the part-time specialist is more productive and requires less supervision than the full-time generalist. The 1970s pattern for the congregation averaging 500 at worship called for four or five full-time program generalists, with two or three of them fully credentialed clergy. The 1990s model calls for the congregation averaging 1,000 at worship to be served by one or two full-time, fully credentialed and full-time ordained generalists, two or three full-time lay specialists, and a dozen to two dozen part-time specialists, one or two of whom may be ordained. The 1990s model costs about 60 to 80 percent of that 1970s model on a per worship attender basis after allowing for the impact of inflation.

In addition to those three variables, nine broad generalizations provide part of the larger context for appraising staff needs. The first of these generalizations is that the economic concept of economy of scale does not apply on a consistent basis in staffing Protestant congregations in North America.

For a congregation with a full-time and fully credentialed resident pastor, the optimum economic size may be an average worship attendance of approximately 140 to 175. Typically these churches are served by a pastor and one-to-four limited part-time persons (custodian, musician, secretary, and possibly a program specialist). As the size goes up, the cost of staffing usually increases at a faster rate than the increase in worship attendance. The economy of scale usually does not reappear until the average worship attendance exceeds 800. The expectations people bring to the churches averaging 300 or 500 or 700 at worship in regard to quality, choices, relevance, music, drama, and specialized ministries tend to be relatively high in cost, but the participation base is too small to produce an economy of scale. In other words, from a strictly financial point of view, those congregations averaging 175 to 700 or so are not the most efficient size for staffing.

A second generalization is that with one big exception, most Protestant congregations in North America would be well advised to examine alternatives other than a full-time and fully credentialed resident pastor. One reason for this statement is the fact that the majority of Protestant congregations on this continent average fewer than seventy-five people at worship. A second reason is the shortage of highly competent ministers who want to spend the next fifteen years serving a small church. The third reason is the emergence of many attractive alternatives for the congregation averaging fewer than 85 to 120 at worship.[5] The big exception to this generalization consists of those smaller congregations with (a) the potential to experience substantial numerical growth, (b) the potential to become the central church for a cluster of small congregations and/or (c) a specialized community ministry.

A third broad generalization is that more staff usually are required in the numerically shrinking congregations than in the numerically growing churches (that largely reflects the twin variables of competence and productivity).

A fourth broad generalization is that those congregations averaging 160 to approximately 700 or more at worship often need one full-time program staff person, or the equivalent in part-time staff, for every 100 average worship attendance. Thus the congregation averaging 400 at worship might be staffed by a full-time pastor, a full-time program director, a half-time administrator, and four or five part-time lay specialists, one part-time ordained person, plus office and custodial staff.

The fifth broad generalization is that the shorter the tenure of program staff, the larger the number who will be needed. A high rate of turnover in the program staff, including the ordained staff, usually means more staff to maintain the same level of productivity. In the ideal world, program staff tenure varies from fifteen to forty years. In the high turnover staff, the median tenure will be closer to seven years.

The sixth broad generalization is that the greater the reliance on electronic data processing, the smaller the office staff. The church secretary is joining the bank teller, the coal miner, the male gynecologist, the male director of Christian education, the stenographer, the farmer, the male bartender, the service station attendant, and the sewing machine operator as endangered species in the American labor force.

The seventh broad generalization is that more staff are required if the goal is to reach nonbelievers and unchurched believers than if most of next year's adult new members will consist of people who have left another congregation to come to this church.

The broad generalization on costs is that the combined total compensation of everyone on the payroll, including housing, pensions, health insurance, continuing education, and workers' compensation, will not exceed one-half of all expenditures. That will leave 10 to 20 percent for routine maintenance of the real estate, 15 to 25 percent for benevolences, and 20 to 30 percent for program including utilities and insurance. The base amount for those percentages does not include expenditures for construction costs or debt service.

The last of these nine generalizations applies to many, but not all, congregations averaging 350 or more at worship. The beginning point for staffing is not adequate support for the current ministry. It is not the staffing of new outreach ministries. The beginning point consists of three questions. First, what is it our senior minister will not do? Second, what is it our senior minister cannot do? Third, who will do what the senior minister or head of staff cannot do or will not do?

In the ideal world, designing a staff configuration begins with the call to do ministry. In the real world, it often begins with the current staff in general and the senior minister in particular.

D. What Are the Criteria and Trends for Designing Our Schedule?

One of the most divisive issues facing many churches today is the hope that they can design a schedule that will please everyone. The self-appraisal task force may choose to begin by identifying the values and the goals on which

the present schedule is based. This can be illustrated by looking quickly at sixteen examples of how values and goals do influence the design of the schedule.

1. *Tradition.* This is the schedule we have always followed here with Sunday school followed by worship.

2. *Placate the building.* When we constructed this building, we promised we would fill it at least once a week. We cannot go to two worship services until after we fill all the seats week after week at one service. We must keep the building happy!

3. *The location in the time zone.* Congregations located near the eastern end of a time zone have a tremendous advantage over those located near the western edge of the time zone. The sun rises an hour earlier at the eastern end of the time zone, and in the winter that is a big difference. It is much easier to begin at 8:00 A.M. or 8:30 A.M. in the north if you are in the eastern end of a time zone. It also should be acknowledged that the National Football League makes it difficult for churches in the western time zone when football doubleheaders on television begin at 10:00 A.M.

4. *Parking.* The availability of both street and off-street parking may be the most influential single factor in designing the Sunday morning schedule.

In many communities the number of automobiles

required to bring one hundred persons on Sunday morning has doubled since 1960. How can we design a schedule that will allow each parking space to be used by at least two vehicles on Sunday morning?

5. *Choices.* In many larger, long-established and highly pluralistic congregations, it has become very important to provide a broad range of meaningful choices for people. This may result in a complex schedule with different members of the same family arriving and departing at different times.

6. *Singing and fellowship.* For some members the most important criterion is the need to fill the pews. They know this strengthens congregational singing. It also enables everyone to see their friends and it does reinforce a sense of unity. How important is that in your church?

7. *Who is your target constituency?* The young parents who seek a one-hour package with worship and children's Sunday school at the same hour? Or mature adults who prefer a two-hour package including both worship and an adult class? Or those families that include teenagers and who seek a two-hour package that provides both Sunday school and worship? Or are we seeking to accommodate that small group of adults who treasure a chance to be in an adult class, to participate in corporate worship, and also to teach a class of children and youth and who prefer a three-hour schedule?

8. *When will the big crowd attend?* In large congregations with two or more worship experiences offered every weekend, when do we prefer to have the largest crowd?

    If we offer two worship experiences on Sunday morning, are we expecting the first service or the second service to have the larger attendance? That decision will influence the choice of the hour for the first service. It also will influence the planning for music, the choice of the

...AND EARLY ON *the* FIRST DAY OF THE WEEK, EVEN BEFORE *the* KICK OFF *of* FOOTBALL GAMES, *the* WOMEN CAME *to* THE TOMB...

Since more Americans are spending less time in bed, earlier worship services are beginning to make sense!

—FRIAR TUCK

preacher, and the format for each service. An increasingly common pattern is to offer two or three or four or five different worship experiences. A nontraditional worship experience designed by and for younger adults may be scheduled for Saturday evening. A traditional service with Holy Communion may be scheduled early on Sunday morning. Concurrently a family worship service may be held in the church parlor. Later on Sunday morning a nontraditional service may be organized around a thirty-five-minute persuasive preaching sermon plus forty minutes of new music, drama, prayer, and the passing of the peace. An increasing number of congregations now offer concurrent worship experiences twice every Sunday morning.

9. In many congregations the most important value questions concern youth and children.

    a. How high a value do we place on planning a schedule that encourages children and youth to participate in *both* Sunday school and corporate worship?

    b. At what age do we encourage young children to attend worship?

    c. What choices do we offer the family that includes a two-year-old child and a seven- or eight-year-old child?

    d. Do we prefer a schedule that encourages the

development of a youth choir without the warm-up period interfering with Sunday school?

  e. If we offer duplicate Sunday school classes for children on Sunday morning, do we want to encourage or discourage children changing back and forth from week to week? What does the discontinuity do to the child's learning experience? To the development of a sense of community in the classes? To the teachers?

  f. Does our schedule suggest to children and youth that Sunday school is more important than corporate worship? If it does, is that a value we want to perpetuate?

10. Thousands of congregations are part of a two-church or three-church parish or yoked field or circuit. What are the values behind their Sunday morning schedules?

  a. Do we place a high value on the ten or fifteen minutes the minister has for pastoral contacts following the close of each worship service? Or is the minister expected to leave immediately following the benediction?

  b. Is the minister expected to lead each worship service from the very beginning or would it be possible for laypersons to serve as liturgists or worship leaders at the second (and third) churches in order to ease the time pressure?

  c. What role is expected of the minister in the Sunday morning church school? Is the schedule consistent with this expectation?

  d. Is it assumed that the congregation paying the largest share of the minister's salary gets first choice on the hour of worship?

  e. Should the longest travel period be after the last Sunday morning service? Or before the first service?

11. In thousands of Protestant congregations the mem-

bers, and especially the longtime members, place a very high value on the time for fellowship.

    a. How much time should we allow for fellowship between Sunday school and worship? If it is too long, will we discourage some persons from attending both worship and Sunday school? How will the newcomers respond?

    b. Or would it be more consistent with our values and goals to plan a fellowship period following worship? What will be the impact on parking needs? Will that help us meet and greet visitors?

    c. How early can we begin in the morning in this time zone in order to provide for an adequate fellowship period later in the morning?

    d. When should we schedule the fellowship period so it will reinforce, rather than compete with other parts of the Sunday morning schedule?

12. Frequently abrasive conflicts emerge around competing demands on the time of adults.

    a. Does your schedule encourage Sunday school teachers to share in corporate worship *and* in the fellowship period?

    b. If you place a high value on *both* adult classes *and* on vocal music, does the schedule encourage or require choir members to leave their classes early in order to provide preparation time for the choir? If so, can that be changed by scheduling the fellowship period for after church school?

    c. If you offer two worship services on Sunday morning, is it possible to have two different choirs rather than expect some members to sing at both services?

    d. Do we want to develop a schedule that encourages and reinforces *continuing* adult classes? Does our schedule do that?

    e. Do we expect adult study groups will meet on Sunday mornings or during the week or both?

    f. Do we want to offer special education classes on Sunday morning for persons with special needs such as the visually handicapped or the hearing impaired or developmentally disabled or the hyperactive child or new Christians or newcomers from a Roman Catholic heritage or newlyweds or new parents or people for whom English is their second language?

13. If we offer two worship services and one has double the attendance of the other, should we (a) accept that as normal and predictable or (b) try to equalize the attendance by a stronger ministry of music at the less attended service and/or by shifting the schedule slightly so the less attended service has a more attractive beginning and ending time?

14. Do we change to a summer schedule for the convenience of our members or do we stay with the same predictable Sunday morning schedule on a year around basis because we know that will facilitate reaching newcomers to the community two-thirds of whom move in between mid-May and the middle of September?

15. Or is our number one goal to attract nonbelievers and unchurched believers to come worship with us on Sunday morning? If that is our top priority, how can we design a schedule to undergird that hope? What does that say when we schedule Holy Communion?

16. Or is our number one value to encourage and support diversity and our number one goal to build an intergenerational and multicultural congregation? How many choices will we have to offer people in music to be consistent with that value and that goal? How

many kinds of worship services will we have to offer every weekend to undergird that value and that goal? How many different preachers will we need every weekend to maintain a high level of diversity? Or do we conclude that the easiest way to accomplish this is to build on (a) a network of one-to-one relationships with a gregarious, extroverted, and personable pastor at the hub of that network, (b) one sixty- to ninety-minute worship experience every weekend, and (c) an average worship attendance in the seventy-five to 125 range?

A different beginning point for the self-appraisal task force is to look at national trends and decide how these should impact the local schedule. This can be illustrated by five trends that surfaced during the closing years of the second millennium.

The first of these is the growing popularity of the four-period schedule for Sunday morning. One reason for this is Americans are spending less time in bed. Related to this is the trend toward going to church earlier on Sunday morning. An increasing number of congregations, especially in the Southwest, are reporting their smallest crowd is at the last worship service on Sunday morning. Another part of the background is more people are eating breakfast away from home. The other big factor is the rise in the demand for the teaching ministry. Add to this mixture the sharp increase in the number of one-person and two-person households, and one result is the four-period schedule that begins with breakfast.

The choir that sings at the 8:30 A.M. service arrives shortly after 7:00 to eat together, socialize, and leisurely make their way to the choir room. Another group of adults go through the serving line and take their trays to a classroom for a two-hour class. Others come to eat and socialize before going to that first worship experience. One or two commit-tees or task forces come early to transact their work over breakfast. One of the fringe benefits is the increase in the size of the crowd at that first worship service.

One variation on this is the four-period schedule that adds brunch to the typical three-period scenario. This is especially popular in those congregations that (a) attract large numbers of young adults who enjoy eating lunch together, and/or (b) attract large numbers of first-time visitors, with all visitors being invit-ed to remain for lunch, and/or (c) include large numbers of mature adults who enjoy one another's company, and (d) sched-ule a variety of events and classes for Sunday afternoon.

A second trend is the result of that rapid increase in the number of large congregations with limited space for worship. This has been reinforced by that growing demand for choices. One result is the schedule that calls for two worship experi-ences at the same hour. The traditional service with tradition-al music usually is held in the sanctuary while the alternative service with contemporary Christian music is held in the chapel, fellowship hall, gymnasium, or family life center.

A recent trend is to offer a seventy-five- to ninety-minute worship service at 5:00 or 5:30 P.M. Saturday that is designed primarily for parents of young children who (a) are coming back to church after a long absence, (b) are in two-income households and want to keep all day Sunday open as a fami-ly time, (c) prefer a church with a strong teaching emphasis in the sermon, and (d) want their young children in the nurs-ery while they worship.

A fourth trend is to offer five to eight *different* worship experiences every weekend with two on Saturday evening, three to five on Sunday morning, one on Sunday late after-noon or evening, and one on Monday evening. This sched-ule is found only in those congregations seeking to reach and serve an exceptionally broad slice of the total population and/or churches with limited physical facilities.

The last of these five recent developments may also be the rarest. In these congregations, one Sunday morning worship experience is designed for the searchers, seekers, and explorers who are at an early stage of their personal religious pilgrimage. A different worship experience is designed for those at a more advanced stage of their faith development. A third is designed for those ready to accept the challenge to become deeply committed disciples of Christ. The second and third may or may not be offered on Sunday morning. One or both may be scheduled for another time, such as midweek or Sunday evening or Saturday evening. Frequently two different worship experiences are offered in different rooms at the same time.

The subversion of goals occurs when attractive means-to-an-end issues take over the agenda. One way to minimize that temptation is to postpone the discussion of these concerns until after thirty or forty other self-appraisal questions have received appropriate study. That is why this chapter comes in the second half of this volume.

CHAPTER SEVEN

How Large Should We Build It?

"We're a seventeen-year-old congregation, and we're ready to build our permanent worship center," explained the founding pastor of a congregation now averaging nearly 700 at worship. "Half of our building planning committee wants a sanctuary that will seat about 1,600. That will enable us to bring everyone together at one time for worship and still leave us room to double in size. The other half of our committee is equally committed to growth, but they are convinced we should continue with two worship experiences on Sunday morning and eventually add a third on Saturday evening, perhaps a fourth on Monday evening, and, possibly, if our growth exceeds our expectations, add a third service to the Sunday morning schedule. They believe if we build to seat 600 or so we could at least double in size with 400 at one service on Sunday morning and 500 at the other, plus 300 on Saturday evening, and another 300 on either Monday evening or at a third service on Sunday morning. What do you think we should do?"

"I can tell you only two things for certain," replied the parish consultant. "First, I don't know what would be a wise decision. Second, I doubt if you can arrive at a wise decision without first addressing at least a score of other questions."

"We don't have time for any more study," replied this pastor. "We've been meeting for over a year and our deadline is the first Tuesday of next month. That is the date of our congregational meeting at which time we'll vote on a building program."

"Well, that's one way to make decisions," commented the consultant. "Let the calendar drive the process. A better way, in my opinion, is to feed more information into the process."

"Okay," conceded the pastor. "What are the questions we should address? Maybe we already have and we are ready to make a decision."

"If you are serious," began the consultant, "you may need to ask a lot of questions. The 'how large should it be?' question is about twenty-second on this list, and that will be easy to answer after you have addressed the first twenty-one. So, here is your list of questions."

Twenty-one Questions

1. Who is your number one constituency for Sunday morning worship?

Your members? Or your first-time visitors? If the answer is first-time visitors, you want a simple building design with a minimum of distractions and your parking focused on the main entrance to your worship center. You will want to create an inviting entrance area and a warm atmosphere, and minimize any design feature that might intimidate a first-time visitor. You design it on the assumption people will follow the same path when they depart that they took to enter. You will locate restrooms to be easily seen and accessible to anyone as they enter or as they depart from the building through that main entrance.

If your primary client is your own members, you will design the building to welcome people who come directly from outside into the building as well as those who are coming from a classroom in your educational wing. That means you will locate restrooms that will be easily accessible to anyone coming from a classroom to worship. The same is true for the location of your cloakrooms. Will they be located near the entrance to the educational wing for members who come first to a class and later go to worship? Or will they be conveniently located for the first-time visitor to worship?

The big distinction is that if you are designing it primarily for first-time visitors on Sunday morning, you probably will not schedule Holy Communion for Sunday morning. If, however, your number one constituency will be your members, you will want to design it to facilitate observance of the Lord's Supper.

2. Who is the primary audience for worship in your church?

If you answer that your number one goal is to design a worship service that will be pleasing to God, you probably will design the space so worshipers enter and depart through the same route.

If, however, your number one goal is to design a worship experience that challenges believers to become disciples, you will seek a different design. You expect the worshipers will be transformed by this experience. That means you will design the space leading into your worship center to affirm the pilgrimage from inquirer to believer to disciple. The route your worshipers will follow when they depart from worship will be designed to challenge disciples to go out into the world as missionaries of Jesus Christ. You do not want transformed disciples to depart following the same route they entered for that life-changing experience.

3. How large a slice of the population do you expect to serve?

If you expect to reach and serve one-half of one percent of the people who live within twenty miles of your meeting place, that could be 2,000 out of a total of 400,000 residents.

That would be consistent with those who want to schedule only one worship service for Sunday morning. If you focus on a very thin slice of the total population, you should be able to build a relatively homogeneous congregation, and one service is compatible with that role.

If, however, you expect to reach and serve 10 percent of the 20,000 people who live reasonably close to your meeting place, that almost certainly will mean a far higher degree of heterogeneity among your people. To serve that more heterogeneous collection of people, you probably should expect to offer two or three or four different worship experiences every weekend. That probably would lead you to design a worship center that will seat 500 to 700, rather than one that will seat 1,500 or more.

4. Do you conceptualize your church as one congregation or as a congregation of congregations?

You now average nearly 700 at worship. Most congregations that reach that size follow one of four paths. The majority attempt to use yesterday as a road map to tomorrow and plateau in size. A small number change pastors and shrink back to a more comfortable size. Perhaps one out of five expand their geographical service area. The same approach to ministry reaches the same percentage of people, but the larger service area means a larger potential constituency and so they continue to grow. Another 20 percent, more or less, reconceptualize themselves as a congregation of congregations, add the appropriate staff, greatly enlarge the group life, create several strong and cohesive organizations within the larger fellowship (a women's organization, a men's organization, a missions council, a youth group, a ministry of music, and so forth), and offer a variety of attractive entry points for potential future members including two or three or four or five or six different worship experiences every weekend. That enables them to continue to grow.

You should choose one of those four paths, make other

decisions that will be consistent with that choice, and design a building to house the path you have chosen.

5. How many excellent preachers will you have on your staff five years from now?

This overlaps the last question. Conceptualizing the identity and role as one very large congregation usually means one person will be the preacher (or speaker or teacher) at all the worship experiences on at least forty weekends a year.

Accepting the role as a congregation of congregations as your road to tomorrow usually requires two or three superb communicators on the preaching staff. Three will speak on thirty weekends annually, two on twenty weekends, and, perhaps, one on two weekends a year.

Frequently the youngest of the three will leave after about seven years to become the senior pastor of another large church and be replaced by a young minister of great promise as a preacher and future senior minister. So, if you plan for one person to do all the preaching on most weekends, you will want to design a very large room for worship. If you expect to have two or three preachers on each weekend, you may have one traditional room for worship that seats perhaps 500 to 800 plus one or two other multipurpose rooms for nontraditional worship experiences.

6. How will you schedule worship?

The traditional pattern has been sequential. A Saturday evening service, an early Sunday morning service, and a late Sunday morning service is a common example.

If the goal is to reach and serve a broader slice of the local population, this may mean offering concurrent worship experiences. The nontraditional experience is scheduled for a room designed with great flexibility in how it is used. The traditional worship service is scheduled for the same time in a traditional environment.

One example of a useful design is based on a schedule calling for five worship services on Sunday morning. Sunday morning begins with breakfast at seven o'clock followed by an early service organized around Holy Communion. Two adult classes meet concurrently, the two or two and one-half hour class began with breakfast, the other began at the same time as the first worship service. These two classes enable adults who want to teach in the Sunday school later and also participate in corporate worship to enjoy a continuing adult class.

The next block of time on the schedule included (1) a traditional worship service in a room designed primarily for worship that will accommodate 300 to 700 worshipers, (2) a nontraditional worship experience in a large multipurpose room, (3) an adult Bible study or Forum class in a room that will seat 300 to 700, usually led by the same exceptionally gifted teacher who may or may not be one of the pastors, and (4) a variety of classes for all ages including at least one other adult class.

The building is designed so the entrance to both worship services and to the room with that huge adult class is off one very large space. This encourages the adults attending either one of the two worship services or that big adult class to socialize with other people before and after that experience. Ideally one corridor leading from that huge central open space leads to one cluster of classrooms and a second corridor leads to another cluster of meeting rooms. Ideally this large room will have a direct entrance from a convenient parking area.

The location of the office area will depend on other design considerations including off-street parking, security, the location of the kitchen, the size of the staff, and the amount of available land.

The schedule for the last block of time on Sunday morning duplicates the previous period, but the design of the two worship experiences may differ greatly from the previous hour.

This schedule and design calls for a minimum of two pastors who are excellent communicators, high energy personalities, and far above average preachers.

Thus two concurrent services early on Sunday morning and two concurrent services later require a smaller worship center than if the schedule calls for only one or two services for that same number of people, but more space may be required for parking and vehicular traffic.

7. Carbon copies or choices?

Will the design of the worship services scheduled for your worship center or sanctuary be the same? Or will they vary greatly? The old pattern called for the second service to be a carbon copy, except perhaps for the music, of the first. The new pattern frequently calls for two or three or four substantially different worship experiences in the same room every weekend.

The old pattern affirmed that the design of the room should dictate both the size of the crowd and the behavior of the people. The new pattern calls for a design that (a) suggests to worshipers the room is comfortably full whether the crowd numbers 300 or 700 and (b) is supportive of and compatible with a variety of forms of worship.

The "Good News at Six O'Clock" service on Sunday evening often displays only a limited resemblance to Sunday morning worship.

8. Oratory or conversation?

The Republican Convention in San Diego in mid-August 1996 presented two radically different styles of communication. One was modeled by Bob Dole who stood on the platform behind a podium to address the crowd in a traditional style of platform oratory. The other was modeled by Elizabeth Dole who walked among the people down on the convention floor and provided a superb example of the effec-

tiveness of one-to-one relational communication. Mr. Dole utilized a radio style, and Mrs. Dole used a television model.

The design of your worship center should reflect your choice between the traditional oratorical style of the radio era or the conversational style of the television age.[1]

9. European or American?

The European tradition for Christian worship calls for a presentation type service led by one or two adults, a relatively passive role for the worshipers, a major role for a performance type vocal choir, a pipe organ, great formality, and considerable liturgy, with God as the number one audience for that event.

The American approach to Christian worship usually assumes a more participatory role for the worshipers, a response to the call to discipleship, a faster pace, a more informal atmosphere, and a larger role for lay leadership in that worship experience.[2]

The European tradition assumes the worship service

should be designed for believers. The American tradition assumes God will be pleased if that worship experience transforms nonbelievers into believers and/or believers into disciples.

Do your plans call for replicating the nineteenth-century European style of worship or the late-twentieth-century American approach? Your design should be supportive of your choice.

10. *What is the scale of your total design?*

Today we have an excess of meeting places for congregations that seat 700 at worship, provide off-street parking for 200 worshipers, accommodate 150 adults in attractive Sunday school classrooms, and seat 200 people at tables in the fellowship hall.

A minimum goal is one off-street parking space for every two seats in the room in which people gather for corporate worship, at least one classroom seat for an adult for every seat in the worship center, and at least one seat at a table in the fellowship hall for every two seats in the worship center. A different criterion is one acre of land for every 100 seats in the worship center.

SADLY, THOSE WHO PLANNED OUR STAIRWAYS NEVER DREAMED of GROWING OLD!

Most folks in any building prefer staying on the same level!

—FRIAR TUCK

11. *Escalators or elevators?*

In many communities the price of land makes it economically feasible to construct a two- or three- or four- or five-story building. The typical design gives people a choice between stairs and a well-concealed elevator.

Shopping malls, airport terminals, and office buildings have been teaching people that the norm is the choice between easily accessible escalators, which are high maintenance items, and elevators, but most people prefer to remain on the same level.

What will you do to persuade people that stairs should be their first preference?

In other words, this has become a one-story world. If you plan to construct a two- or three- or four- or five-story building, how will this affect the design for your place of worship?

12. How will you provide good sight lines?

The basic choice is between the sloping floor and a low platform versus a flat floor and a high platform. What is your preference?

Which will provide the greatest flexibility in use? Which will be the most difficult to remodel twenty years from now when a new generation decides they want to do church differently? Which is the easier and less expensive in providing people with a choice of exits? Which is most compatible with the European approach to worship? With the American approach? Which will be least intimidating to adults past seventy years of age? Which creates the appropriate atmosphere for the approach to worship that you plan to offer?

13. Do you plan to televise your worship services?

If not, do you want to build that in as an easy option for future generations? Or do you prefer to make it difficult for that to ever happen?

If you plan to televise your worship services, will they be taped, edited, and telecast later? Or do you plan on a live telecast?

What does that answer say to the pace of your live worship experiences? What does that say to your design?

14. *Spoken words or musical sounds?*

Will the design of your worship center place the higher priority on transmitting the spoken word? Or of musical sounds? How will you compensate for the other?

15. *Acoustic or electronic?*

Will the design call for a heavy emphasis on the acoustic sound in music? Or on the electronic sound? Will your design reflect that decision?

16. *Vocal choir or worship team?*

Do you plan to schedule worship services with a large and highly visible performance type vocal choir? Where will they be seated? To be easily visible to a congregation of passive worshipers? Or in a balcony to the rear where they can reinforce congregational singing? Or split between two side balconies to provide an antiphonal sound? Which drives the selection of singers and instrumentalists in the ministry of music? High quality performance? Or the rapid assimilation of newcomers? If the answer is performance, what are your backup systems for assimilating newcomers? (Musical groups often are the most effective channel for quickly assimilating 10 to 20 percent of all adult newcomers. If that is not a high priority for the ministry of music, what will replace it?)

Or does your worship design call for an orchestra and/or band and six to twenty worship leaders? Will the preacher also serve as a worship leader? Or have limited visibility until the time comes to speak? Will your design accommodate a range of options in this facet of ministry?

17. *Video or oral announcements?*

Will announcements be made orally by individuals? Or by video projection? Do you plan for rear projection, or for reflected images on the screen? Will these screens be used for

Do you want baptisms
separated from
the congregation
or viewed by everyone?
—FRIAR TUCK

HERE'S TWO MORE
DOWN FRONT!!

Movable chairs
can help accommodate
any size congregation!
—FRIAR TUCK

other forms of communication during worship? Will you need more than one screen? More than one video projector? If you do not plan now for video projection, do you want to make it difficult and expensive to be installed later? Will the design for natural light in that new worship center be compatible with daytime video projection?

18. Where and how will baptisms be conducted?

Do you want this to be a ritual that can be easily viewed by everyone? Or do you want substantial physical separation between the person being baptized and the worshipers?

19. What will be the seating arrangements?

Do you plan for fixed pews that are fastened to the floor? Or movable pews? Or theater seats? Or movable chairs so you can adjust the amount of available seating to the anticipated size of the crowd? Will the chancel furnishings be fixed in place? How much flexibility in seating do you want to build in for tomorrow's worshipers?

The European heritage calls for a fixed design that can be altered only at great expense. The American tradition is to optimize the degree of flexibility so the next generations will enjoy an optimal amount of freedom to make changes.

20. Is this to be a monument to honor the past?

Literally thousands of houses of worship across America have been constructed to fulfill one or more of these dreams, (a) the final phase of a master plan originally prepared decades earlier for a different generation of worshipers, (b) as a monument to the dreams of that long-tenured pastor who needed the ego fulfillment of a new sanctuary that would be completed before the pastor's retirement—or soon after, (c) a beautiful building that could grace the cover of the Sunday bulletins, (d) a room designed to house a magnificent pipe organ, (e) the goal of housing worship services that would replicate the eighth-century European worship that was so pleasing to God, (f) a taller steeple than any other church building in town, (g) a declaration to the larger community that this congregation has arrived and is a force to be reckoned with every day of the week, (h) a monument to an exceptionally generous donor, and (i) an impressive and attractive front entrance facing a busy street to witness to passing motorists.

21. How much should it cost?

One other basic question that must be addressed before deciding on the size of that room is one that almost certainly was asked earlier. What can we afford? The best answer is the new house of worship will be completely paid for somewhere between the day it is ready for occupancy and seven years later.

"Why not spread payments over twenty years?" challenges someone. "That is what many people do when they buy a house. Some people even take out a thirty-year mortgage when they purchase a new home. Would it not be appropriate to take out a twenty-year mortgage and let the users pay for it? Why saddle today's members with most of the cost? After all, this building probably will be used for worship for at least fifty or a hundred years."

That is a frequently asked question and deserves a response. Among the reasons for a comparatively brief mortgage payment schedule, five stand out.

First, paying off a big mortgage can become the number one concern of a congregation. Twenty-five years ago a California minister, Charles Lee Wilson, wrote a wonderful description of how this can become a subversion of purpose.

> We built a new building and we agreed to make payments of $1,900 each and every month for a long period of time—and some of us spoke of that payment that always followed us as the "wolf."

> Some months we fell behind in our payments and we felt the wolf snapping at our heels, but every year as the wolf followed us up and down our monthly hills and valleys we would put on a blinding burst of speed and close our year panting gratefully, We made it again!

> Somewhere along the years, we said, we have lived with this wolf so closely and so long that we ought to make a pet of him. However, it wasn't until we finished the debt and said, farewell to you, wolf that we realized what a likable pet he really was. He gave us direction like, which way shall we go? Here comes the wolf, let's go to the closest spot to find a payment. He gave us motivation—man, we've got to make another payment or we are in trouble with the wolf. The wolf also gave us a wonderful excuse for anything we didn't get around to—if it took time, money, or action, we could whiz by saying, "I made my payment and my business is staying ahead of the wolf."

> For so long, we could hate the wolf, blame the wolf, enjoy beating the wolf, tell each other scary wolf stories and everything right up until we paid the mortgage and waved farewell to the wolf. We paid off the mortgage with such enthusiasm that we had $3,000 left over. We might have done it a year ago

but we got a new organ and bought a lot instead. The $10,000 payment on the total purchase price of the lot was sort of like a wolf cub cute and a little like daddy. In fact, when we got through with the debt and had $3,000 left, we gave it all to the lot so the little wolf would be two years ahead on his diet.[3]

ALL WE ARE, OR EVER WILL BE, WE OWE to THE WOLF!

HOWL! GULP!

BANK PAYMENT DUE!

Large and long mortgages promote overbuilding, inadequate staffing, and few options!
—FRIAR TUCK

Second, unlike a family purchasing a home, the congregation moving into a new building often resembles a passing parade of people. Seven to ten years after completing the building, one-half of the members are people who were not involved in designing nor in deciding to construct that new building. Frequently they display little interest in paying off a mortgage contracted by someone else long before they came on the scene.

Third, those monthly mortgage payments can cause a congregation to focus on the past, to second guess the decisions of that earlier building planning committee, and to put means-to-an-end issues above ministry in the local agenda. A short-term mortgage makes it easier to focus on ministry and on the challenges tomorrow will bring.

Fourth, a willingness to take on a big mortgage to be paid off over twenty or more years often (a) encourages overbuilding, (b) produces an excessive long delay before the program staff can be expanded to meet the needs of a larger congregation, and (c) limits the options open to the next generation of leaders. Far too many mortgage payments are being met from the salaries not paid to staff who were not hired because of those big mortgage payments. That white elephant must be fed every month.

Finally, the best legacy this generation of leaders can leave to the next generation is the optimal level of flexibility to be able to adapt to changing times. That generalization applies to both the design of that new building and to the plan to pay for it.

The best legacy leaders can leave is future flexibility!

—FRIAR TUCK

After you have agreed on the answers to those twenty-one questions, it will be relatively easy to decide how big that new worship center should be.

What Else?

This is not offered as a comprehensive word on design, only on the question of size. In the overall design many other questions should be raised. For example, does the design include at least one low visibility exit from the chancel or stage? Will the doors in the main entrance be made of wood or steel to keep people out? Or of glass to invite people to come in? Will the design include one large parking lot for all vehicles? Or will each entrance be marked by a pod of convenient parking spaces? Where will vehicles be stored as the drivers wait to exit onto the street? Will the staff office wing include at least one conference room that can accommodate at least fifteen people comfortably? Will the design of the structure silently direct people where to find the room or activity they seek?

Or will many interior signs be required? Will a stranger coming on Tuesday morning know the correct door to enter? Will the kitchen be designed to make it easy for a caterer to work there? Will the design increase or reduce problems of security and vandalism? Will the design encourage an efficient use of energy?

These are examples of other questions that should be raised about the overall design of a new building.[4]

Three Fork-in-the-Road Questions

A serious and in-depth self-appraisal effort usually will raise at least a couple of complicated fork-in-the-road questions. A common example is the pastor who asks, "Should I plan to continue here for another decade or longer, or has the time come for me to move on?" A second is the congregation that debates, "Should we invest more money in this functionally obsolete building on this small site or should we relocate the meeting place to larger facilities?" In another church the leaders are torn between continued numerical growth and planting a new daughter church every year or two. A fourth is when the members in what was founded as a neighborhood parish in 1923 have difficulty in deciding between attempting to reach the recent newcomers to that neighborhood, many of whom represent a substantially different slice of the population, or accepting a role as a regional church. In a different congregation the debate finds one group wanting to add staff to better serve today's members and their children while others contend the new staff should concentrate on reaching the unchurched.

Those are among the more common fork-in-the-road

questions that emerge from the self-appraisal process. While they are less widely discussed than the issues mentioned here, the changing societal context for doing ministry has created a need to look at three other fork-in-the-road questions.

A. Teaching or Learning?

A central theme of American Protestantism has been to teach people what they should know about the Bible, Christian doctrine, how to be a better Christian, and church (and denominational) history. Among the many expressions of this have been the two-hour sermons of the seventeenth, eighteenth, and nineteenth centuries, the founding of hundreds of Christian colleges, the Sunday school movement, the decision in several traditions to require both a college degree and a seminary degree for ordination, a growing number of continuing education events for both the clergy and the laity, vacation Bible school, confirmation classes, the construction of hundreds of thousands of Sunday school classrooms, the recent increase in the number of Protestant Christian day schools, the hundreds of millions of dollars contributed to theological seminaries and divinity schools,[1] recent translations of the Bible designed to be read by the laity, the use of television as a teaching tool by hundreds of churches,

HER CHARACTER, COMMITMENT, COMPETENCE, and CALL ARE BETTER THAN MY CREDENTIALS!

—FRIAR TUCK

Many growing churches choose their program staff from their current members!

and the recent increase in the number of high-expectation adult Bible study programs.

Most of these efforts were designed from a producer's perspective. This is what you ought to know and this is what we are prepared to teach you.

This focus on teaching has been paralleled in public schools and in institutions of higher education. In recent years, however, a growing discontent has surfaced with the public schools. Elementary and high school students are not learning what parents and employers believe they should know. More recently, parallel criticisms have been raised about what students in institutions of higher education are or are not learning.

One response by the discontented consumers is the recent rapid increase in the number of parents who have chosen the home schooling option. A second is the increasing number of employers who offer on-the-job learning experiences for employees. Motorola Corporation, McDonalds, and General Motors are among the nationally emulated examples. A third response is the growing number of larger congregations who choose program staff from among the current membership. Their emphasis is on qualities such as character, Christian commitment, the call to ministry, and competence rather than on academic credentials.

WHAT I THINK YOU NEED *to* KNOW, ISN'T NECESSARILY SO!

Today, local churches are better at determining their learning needs than their pastors!

— FRIAR TUCK

Perhaps the most significant response by congregational leaders was stimulated by the book, *The Fifth Discipline* by Peter Senge. Senge's concept of learning communities[2] has been adapted by churches scattered all across the theological spectrum. Among other changes this requires a radical shift in how ministries are designed. Three different beginning points are illustrated by the experiences of three congregations. These examples also illustrate several of the central characteristics of a learning community.

One August, most of the members of a Sunday school class composed of mature adults spent three hours with a dozen teenagers from the eleventh and twelfth grade Sunday school class. The initiative for this meeting came from a grandmother who earlier had suggested, "Instead of rotating the teaching among the members of our class, why don't we ask a couple of teenagers to teach our class?" After six months of discussion, this August meeting was scheduled.

One result was an agreement that in the fall quarter four teams of teenagers, with three-to-five persons on each team, would concentrate on designing the curriculum for that adult class for the winter quarter. During the winter term, each team would have three or four Sundays to teach their unit. In the balance of the winter quarter, these teams would design the curriculum for their unit to be taught in the spring quarter.

A second result was the definition of the themes for these eight units. They were the Christian view of God, death,

> GUESS WHO IS TEACHING WHOM?
>
> —FRIAR TUCK
>
> Today, Christian education needs to be taught intergenerationally!

I GUESS I WENT TOO FAR WITHOUT ASKING *for* FEEDBACK!

Pastors wanting a teaching-preaching ministry need laity to help design their sermon themes!

marriage, church membership, angels, the responsibilities of Christians to the poor, divorce, and evangelism.

A third result was the members of that adult class agreed to find their own teachers for the fall quarter, but that class would be taught by teams of teenagers in the winter and spring quarters.

In another congregation, after five years of preaching nearly identical sermons based on the lectionary at the two Sunday morning worship services, the pastor met with an informal self-appointed group of seven members. "We would like to talk with you about some sermon topics," explained the spokesperson for this group. "Would you be open to the idea of preaching on these topics at the early service and follow that with a sermon feedback discussion during the Sunday school hour?"

Three meetings later an agreement was reached that for ten consecutive weeks (1) the sermon at the first service would speak to an issue raised by the laity, (2) the pastor would schedule the specific Sunday for each theme, (3) a changing group of five to seven volunteers would meet with the pastor for two hours every Monday evening for a time of Bible study on the theme designated for the sermon thirteen days later, and preliminary work on an outline for that sermon, (4) a layperson would lead the discussion during the Sunday school following the preaching of that sermon so that the pastor could be free to participate fully in that discussion, (5) the first five themes for this new series would be forgiveness, life after death, sin, grace, and prayer, (6) while everyone in the congregation would be invited to suggest themes for the second half of this series, this ad hoc group and the pastor would meet together to reduce the number to five, (7) the pastor would be free to preach this same sermon at the second service or to continue to be guided by the lectionary for the sermon at that service, and (8) six weeks after the last week in this series, the pastor and this ad hoc group would meet together to evaluate the results of this experiment.

"Pastor, my husband and I have a problem," explained a mother to her pastor one Tuesday evening after a committee meeting. "Our daughter, Rebecca, is in the third and fourth grade Sunday school class here, and it seems that the teachers run out of time before they finish the lesson. On the way home Rebecca tells us, 'The bell rang before our teacher finished the story and she told us to run along and ask our parents to tell us the rest of that Bible story. Mommy, will you tell me what happened next?' About half the time I can be of some help, but my husband knows even less about the Bible than I do. Is there any way you can persuade the teachers to finish the lesson before the end of the class period?"

A couple of days later that creative pastor suggested an alternative solution to this

Adult Classes

SHE'S BURNING THE MIDNIGHT OIL TO ANSWER HER FIVE-YEAR OLD'S QUESTIONS!

Who ever knows enough?

—FRIAR TUCK

CHILDREN WILL NOT BE SEEN OR HEARD UNLESS THEY'RE BROUGHT!

Attracting adults is a sure way to keep children on track !

FRIAR TUCK

problem. "Beginning a week from next Sunday, we will be offering a new adult Sunday school class. It is designed for parents with children in our third and fourth grade class. The focus of the class will be on the lesson that will be taught in the third and fourth grade class the following week. We want to enable the parents to talk with their children about the lesson both on the way to church, or earlier, and afterward."

Lest there be any misunderstanding, none of these congregations represent a full scale learning community. These experiences are described here for four reasons. First, together they illustrate several of the qualities of a healthy, challenging, and vital learning community. These include shared intergenerational learning experiences, the use of teams, learning by doing, a focus on the needs of the learner rather than largely or entirely on what the teacher has to offer, two-way communication, the use of both highly structured and unstructured learning environments, the importance of adults modeling for younger people the value and joy of learning, and a supportive environment for creativity.

Second, all three experiences illustrate what can be an initial step in a longer and more complex process of evolving from that traditional producer's agenda approach followed by most teaching institutions, including Christian churches, to a greater involvement of the consumers or learners.

Third, all three experiences also illustrate a crucial tactic in the process of planned change. Whenever possible, make incremental changes by addition, not by destroying the status quo.[3]

Children and youth are influenced by what they see adults doing!

Fourth, and some will insist this is the number one quality of a learning community, the most powerful pedagogical tool with children and youth is modeling. Children and youth are influenced by what they see adults doing. One example of this is the congregation that offers excellent Sunday school classes for kids age three through high school, but has no adult Sunday school classes. The lesson being taught is structured learning experiences in the Christian faith on Sunday morning are for children and youth. One of the rewards for reaching adulthood (currently perceived by many teenagers as getting a driver's license) is the right to stop attending Sunday school.

At the other end of that spectrum is the building designed so that children drop off their parents at the appropriate Sunday school classroom and then go to their classes—the three-year-olds follow the yellow brick linoleum floor covering to their three-year-old room, the four-year-olds follow the red line on the wall to their four-year-old room, the five-year-olds follow the blue line on the wall to their five-year-old room, and the first-graders follow the green line to their room. Approximately an hour later, the children return to pick up their parents and go on to worship. Among the lessons taught are (1) everyone enjoys the opportunity to learn, (2) adults often are reluctant to leave that place of learning because they enjoy the experience, (3) everyone is expected to gather together for corporate worship, and (4) adults model for children the norms for churchgoing Christians.

Does your congregation function as a producer-oriented teaching institution? Or does it reflect an increasing number of the qualities of a healthy learning community?

B. Youth or Families?

Perhaps the clearest dividing line among the Protestant churches on this continent is not denominational affiliation or music or size or place on the theological spectrum or the day of the week people gather to worship God or whether they are lay led or clergy led. The clearest dividing line may be between those who (a) focus on youth as a discrete and separate category and (b) those who focus on families that include teenagers.

This point can be illustrated by looking briefly at four different definitions of contemporary reality. The first, shared by the vast majority of public school administrators, nearly all Protestant congregations, many parents, and most denominational agencies, is to define youth as a category and subdivide that huge category by age and grade. Many confirmation classes, Sunday school systems, youth programs, and parachurch organizations begin by dividing youth into smaller groups on the basis of age and grade.

A second perspective is widely shared by most psychiatrists, the scouts for major league baseball teams, family counselors, law enforcement officials, the recruiters for university football and basketball teams, a small but growing number of professionals in youth ministries, and a rapidly growing proportion of elementary school principals. They agree there is a low ceiling on what any adult can do to work with or help a child or teenager without first getting acquainted with that child's (or teenager's) total family constellation.

IF THEY NO LONGER HEAR US, WHO ARE THEY LISTENING TO?

YOUTH LOUNGE

ADULTS STAY OUT!

—FRIAR TUCK

Peer groups now give youth their values, goals, and rules for ethical behavior!

A third perspective is shared by a small but growing number of youth counselors, elementary school principals, the officers and enlisted personnel for indoctrinating new recruits into military service, and by the majority of teenagers. All agree that age and grade in school are not the best lines of demarcation for subdividing children and youth into smaller groups. One example is the elementary school that has replaced the two kindergarten, two first grade, and two second grade classes with six classes, each one including five-, six-, and seven-year-olds.

When asked for their lines of demarcation, teenagers usually rank nationality, language, race, culture, ethnicity, family income, employment during the school year, use of tobacco, kinship ties, home environment, gender, participation in competitive sports, friendship circles, religion, use of hard drugs, dress, and plans for future education ahead of age and grade as they divide the high school population into smaller categories.

A fourth perspective is to compare the world of those who were born in the United States in the 1914–42 era with the world of those who were born after 1968. The older generation was heavily influenced by (1) the national origins of parents; (2) the family environment; (3) small public schools that

IT'S TIME *to* DUST OFF *and* CLEAN UP OUR NURSERIES!

OOPS!

BAWL ROOM

In the '90s, the drop outs of the past two decades are returning as parents!

— FRIAR TUCK

were run by the teachers and the principal; (4) the parents' church affiliation; (5) the value system of that era that taught respect for authority, the merits of deferred gratification, patriotism, and long-term relationships; (6) the Sunday school and other voluntary associations largely managed by adults such as Scouting and 4H Clubs, which affirmed institutional loyalties and traditional standards of ethical behavior; (7) an evangelical Protestant value system that permeated society and affirmed thrift, frugality, Christian standards of ethical behavior, cooperation, and deferred gratification; (8) radio personalities, newspapers, and magazines that reinforced the view this is a typographic society; (9) the Great Depression; (10) the most popular war in American history; (11) survival goals; (12) motion pictures; (13) a national respect for the value of education; and (14) a society that taught the world offers people two choices—take it or leave it.

By contrast, the generations born after 1968 have been heavily influenced by television in general and MTV in particular. Both teach that this is not a typographic society, but rather a world filled with rapidly moving and highly colorful visual images that are accompanied by music. This generation also has been influenced by the comparative affluence of the society into which it was born, which tempts people with a bewildering array of attractive choices; by motion pictures, television programs, and popular music that rank immediate satisfaction above deferred gratification; and by investigative reporting that challenges the authority and morality of traditional institutions (the presidency, universities, financial institutions, the churches, the family, public schools, political parties, and marriage). Peer groups have replaced adult-run organizations as the primary reference point for values, goals, and standards for ethical behavior. Television and peers often are more influential than mothers in a fifteen-year-old

WE'VE GOT A BETTER MENU THAN *the* LOCAL DRIVE-IN!

YOUTH PROGRAM
• BIBLE STUDY
  6 AM - MONDAYS
• MUSIC REHEARSALS
  5 PM - TUESDAYS
• OPEN GYM
  6-10 PM - WEDNESDAYS
• CHESS CLUB
  3 P.M. - THURSDAYS
• PEER GROUP SELF-HELP
  3-8 PM - FRIDAYS
• HABITAT-ALL-DAY
  SATURDAYS

To reach the vast majority of our potential youth, we need a variety of approaches!
—FRIAR TUCK

girl's preference in clothing. The telephone and E-mail have replaced the ancient art of letter writing.

The society into which this generation was born has replaced the heroes of history, legend, and public life with the contemporary heroes of popular music, professional sports, and entertainment. When asked where they see an emphasis on quality, they find this in competitive sports, band, automobiles, clothing, the fast-food restaurant where they work, advanced placement classes in high school, and an occasional teacher but rarely mention church, family, home, or the typical classroom experience. The influence of parental authority has been eroded by a greater emphasis on individualism, do your own thing, and personal self-fulfillment.

Denis P. Doyle has noted that when Japanese parents are asked for the reasons for academic success, they invariably reply, "Effort, hard work, diligence." When Americans are asked the same question, they reply, "Native ability, aptitude, talent, luck."

At least two-thirds of the current generation of high school youth display a powerful consumer orientation, place immediate satisfactions above deferred gratification on their scale of values, are not strongly task-oriented, exhibit limited respect for authority, tend to be obese, are more tolerant of nonconformity, do not demonstrate an automatic acceptance of responsibility for the consequences of one's own actions, display limited respect for other persons and property, tend to be laid back or relaxed, are not driven by the clock and calendar, score lower on tests of verbal skills than previous generations, and are more likely to see their jobs rather than their classroom experiences as the most important source of meaningful self-evaluation.

As you appraise the ministries with children and teenagers in your congregation, what do you do? One alternative is to continue to perceive children as one category of the population and youth as another. A second is to focus on the approximately 30 percent of today's teenagers who can be classified as conventional or straight arrow or traditional. This group displays a greater resemblance to the generations born before 1943 than to the other members of the current generation of teenagers. How do you minister to this generation? Ignore 70 percent and concentrate on the other 30 percent?

A third alternative is the possibility of substituting "with" or "to" in designing ministries with this genera-

CONTRARY to POPULAR OPINION, FOLKS ARE COMING EARLIER AND STAYING LATER . . .

Adult classes, complete Sunday schools, and children in worship are fashionable again!

—FRIAR TUCK

tion. One example of this is the shift from adult leadership for youth ministries to the peer model. Instead of building the leadership team around one to seven adults, several teenagers are identified, enlisted, and trained to provide the necessary leadership.

For some readers the most threatening implication may be in the current actuarial tables. These suggest that most of today's teenagers will outlive contemporary leaders born before 1950. If that turns out to be true, most churches will be faced with four scary alternatives, (a) dissolve, (b) shrink drastically in size, (c) concentrate on that 30 percent of this generation who are comfortable with traditional approaches to congregational life or, (d) change.

A fifth alternative begins with the assumption that only rarely will 100 percent of this generation of teenagers actively support any one goal, program, or priority. One alternative is to be happy with a 25 to 35 percent level of participation. A better alternative is to offer choices and seek, with this cafeteria approach, to reach 50 or 70 or 80 percent of the potential participants through a variety of events, ministries, and programs.

The most challenging alternative is to reconceptualize this as a package of ministries with families that include teenagers. One attractive beginning point for this approach is to begin by designing ministries with families that include children birth to age three. A year or

WHY NOT LET OUR FAMILIES
LEARN AND GROW
OLD TOGETHER ?

—FRIAR TUCK

Letting our families develop our curriculum may be today's educational breakthrough!

two later expand that with a new ministry with families that include children age three to seven. A couple of years later add the ages seven to ten component, and subsequently add the ministries with families with preteens and teenagers.

Finally, a critical implication is to place less emphasis on the spoken and printed word in communicating the gospel and give greater weight to visual communication, music, drama, participation, and symbols.

Another alternative is to hope next year will turn out to be a carbon copy of 1955.

C. How Many in a Group?

When leaders are asked to describe the size of their congregation, using average worship as the yardstick for measuring size, the most common response in American Protestantism is "Between thirty and forty." In several denominations that response will be twice or three times as frequent as "Between twenty and thirty" or "About fifty to sixty" or "Ninety to a hundred" or "Slightly over 100."

How many players is a major league baseball team permitted to carry on its roster? The answer is forty in the winter and twenty-five when the games begin to count.

How many voices are there in that adult church choir on a typical Sunday morning in the congrega-

BEFORE WE STARTED MEETING, I DIDN'T CARE IF I CAME, GAVE, or EVEN BELONGED!

QUESTERS MEET HERE EVERY THURSDAY at 8 P.M.

—FRIAR TUCK

Small groups can raise a church's commitment level!

tion that averages 250 to 700 at worship? About thirty to forty.

What do most public school teachers and administrators agree is the absolute maximum (not ideal, but maximum) number of children in one elementary school class? About thirty to forty.

What is the common size for the second smallest unit in a military unit? For centuries the answer has been twenty-five to forty soldiers.

What is the most common size for a street gang? Six to forty members.

How large is the governing board in those congregations that favor a large board? Rarely more than twenty-five to forty members. What is the typical attendance in the high school youth group meetings in the larger congregations? Typically twenty-five to forty teenagers. What is the attendance in that adult Sunday school class? Rarely more than forty. How many women attend the monthly or quarterly general meetings of the women's organization? Typically twenty-five to forty.

These are but a few of the many examples that can be used to illustrate the Rule of Forty. The theory of group life suggests that there are four basic sizes for groups. One is the small face-to-face group. Nearly every researcher on small-group dynamics reports that when a group includes more than seven persons, that marks the beginning of the erosion of some of the beneficial dynamics of the small group. Eight begins the point of diminishing returns.[4] That is one reason why most committees naturally consist of five or seven persons.

The next size can be described as the overgrown small group. If the members are well acquainted with one another and see one another at least once or twice a week, this group, which usually ranges between eight and seventeen members, can benefit from many of the advantages of small-group dynamics. This is the most common size for the basic unit in a military organization. The value of this size is illustrated by the nine players on a baseball team, the eleven players on a football team, or the basketball squad that usually includes from nine to twelve players. It also is the most common size for a church choir, the attendance in a circle of the women's organization, the typical high school youth group, the membership of the church council or vestry or session, the number of active members in the book circle, or the number of participants in a prayer cell.[5]

For most of us, fifteen or sixteen is the maximum number of persons we can keep track of in our head, recall their names without hesitation, and relate to in a comfortable manner. When the group exceeds seventeen, it is easy for someone to be absent without being noticed, and it is difficult for everyone to be able to have an active role in the discussion. (If each person speaks for only two minutes at a time, that means a participant can speak only four times in a two-hour meeting with fifteen participants.)

The third of these four sizes of groups can be identified as a middle-sized group and typically will include up to thirty-five or forty participants. This is when the Rule of Forty begins to have an impact. That is about as large as a group can become with the relationships of the members to one another as the basic organizing principle. When the size of the group passes twenty to thirty, most of the techniques, procedures, and principles used to strengthen cohesion in a small group lose their value or relevance. These include use of the circle as the basic seating arrangement, asking the participants to take a minute or two each to introduce themselves to the entire group, encouraging everyone to share actively in the discussion, expecting each member to relate to all of the other members of the group, and assuming that each member will develop a strong loyalty or attachment to the group.

The group of thirty to forty members will function most effectively if the responsibilities for leadership are clearly stated and delegated to one or two or three individuals. By contrast, most groups of three to seven persons can function comfortably with either (a) no one person designated as the leader or (b) with a convenor or facilitator who does not pretend to serve as the leader.

This middle-sized group is the transitional size between the overgrown small group and the large group. The Rule of Forty suggests that it is rare for the middle-sized group to be able to include more than forty active participants on a continuing basis.

The large group consists of more than thirty-five to forty participants. The focal point of the large group tends to be on the leader and/or on the task, not on the relationships of the members to one another. When the size of the group passes forty members, three basic changes should be noted. First, absenteeism or dropping out or irregular attendance tends to increase. Second, many of the principles, techniques, and methods that are very effective with groups of fewer than two dozen members begin to become counterproductive. Third, and most important, whenever a class or a choir or a group or an organization includes more than forty participants, it usually is appropriate to discard small-group techniques and replace them with large-group management tools and methods.

If the Rule of Forty is recognized as a natural and predictable phenomenon of organizational life, it can have several useful implications for church leaders.

The first, obviously, is as a diagnostic tool. This Rule of Forty can be a useful criterion for the congregational self-appraisal task force as it examines the life and ministry of each group within that church. For example, one congregation has nearly eighty high school age members, but only thirty-five to forty participate in the youth program. Why? Perhaps because it is organized on middle-sized group principles rather than by utilizing large-group principles?

Second, the leaders in those congregations in which there are several groups, classes, and choirs that have leveled off with an active membership of two to three dozen regular participants have three basic choices. They can be content with their status quo. They may decide to expand the number of small and middle-sized groups, with the expectation that some will stabilize in the eight to seventeen member range and others will plateau in the middle-sized group. Or, third, they may introduce large-group techniques and procedures to enable some of the middle-sized groups to grow into large groups.

A third implication of the Rule of Forty can be seen by looking at those groups that fluctuate in size between thirty-five and forty-five participants. A common example in the larger churches is the chancel choir. Very few adult choirs include more than fifty voices, but many include thirty-five or forty-five voices and appear to violate the Rule of Forty. A closer examination usually reveals that the choir director is utilizing several of the tools appropriate to large groups. Examples include (a) going beyond membership in the choir to requiring a commitment from each member to the common task, such as the special Easter anthem, (b) accepting a very strong leadership role for the choir director, (c) projecting a long time frame for planning, and (d) building on the ability by the choir director to utilize large group principles.

Without a shift to a greater reliance on large-group techniques, however, that choir probably will continue to fluctuate in size between thirty-five and forty-five voices on Sunday morning.

Fourth, for those larger congregations with more than a couple of hundred people at Sunday morning worship, the Rule of Forty suggests it may be useful to have someone on the staff who is knowledgeable about the care and feeding of large groups.[6]

Finally, an awareness of the Rule of Forty can be a useful concept when a congregation is interviewing a candidate for the position of youth director or program director; when a smaller congregation finds itself in a cycle of rapid growth; when the church is contemplating a building program; when the leaders are preparing a church growth strategy; or when the leaders in the women's organization are planning the general meetings for next year. In each case the time has come to consider the value of large groups in the church and the need to utilize large-group techniques in the care and feeding of groups that include sixty or eighty or more participants.

Does the Rule of Forty appear to be a fork-in-the-road issue in your congregation? Are you relying too heavily on small and middle-sized groups and failing to build more large groups? A useful rule-of-thumb is that for every 100 people at worship on the typical weekend, that congregation will have one large group that meets at least forty times a year. In the congregation averaging 500 at worship that might include one adult Sunday school class with an average attendance of 75 to 200; a high school youth group with a regular attendance by 50 to 100 teenagers; perhaps a chancel choir with 45 to 75 active members; possibly two or three dozen teams of three to five per team who are engaged in off-campus ministries on Sunday morning and meet for ninety to 100 minutes at 4:00 P.M. every Sunday afternoon for a time of worship, singing, sharing, inspiration, prayer, fellowship, and mutual accountability; a Tuesday evening worship experience designed for new believers with an average attendance of 75 to 100; the 60 members of the prayer network who meet for an hour every Thursday evening; and the group of 60 to 75 men who are PromiseKeepers who gather at 7:00 A.M. every Saturday morning.

If you and your congregational self-appraisal task force have responded to all these questions, you now should be far beyond denial and ready and eager to begin planning for a new tomorrow for your church as it enters the new millennium. Sic'em!

1. Where Do We Begin?

1. A more extensive discussion of various planning models can be found in Lyle E. Schaller, *Create Your Own Future!* (Nashville: Abingdon Press, 1991), pp. 58-81. While not designed for a religious audience, for a superb book on initiating change see John P. Kotter, *Leading Change* (Boston: Harvard Business School Press, 1996).

2. Witold Rybizynski, *Waiting for the Weekend* (New York: Viking Press, 1991), p. 74.

3. For a somewhat nostalgic reflection on an era when people were more likely to accept and fulfill social expectations, see that provocative book by Alan Ehrenhalt, *The Lost City* (New York: Basic Books, 1995).

4. The pioneering book is by Theodore Levitt, *Innovations in Marketing* (New York: McGraw-Hill Book Company, 1962).

5. This growing trend of creating off-campus ministries is described in Lyle E. Schaller, *Innovations In Ministry* (Nashville: Abingdon Press, 1994), pp. 86-97.

6. Anyone wishing to explore this option could begin by reading Ronald Kotulak, *Inside the Brain* (Kansas City:

Andrews and McNeal, 1996) and subscribe to *Early Childhood Connections*, P.O. Box 4274, Greensboro, NC 27404-4272.

7. For a more extensive discussion of why small congregations tend to project different expectations of their pastor than do large churches, see Lyle E. Schaller, *The Small Membership Church* (Nashville: Abingdon Press, 1994), pp. 23-39.

8. For a brief, lucid, and useful analysis of a new breed of "Made in America" Protestant congregations, see Charles Trueheart, "The Next Church," *The Atlantic Monthly*, August 1996, pp. 37-58. For a revolutionary and challenging description of the new institutional expression of the worshiping Christian community, see Thomas G. Bandy, *Kicking Habits* (Nashville: Abingdon Press, 1996).

9. For a longer discussion of the differences between the European religious heritage and the American religious culture, see Lyle E. Schaller, *The Interventionist* (Nashville: Abingdon Press, 1997), chapter 7.

10. George G. Hunter III, *Church for the Unchurched* (Nashville: Abingdon Press, 1995).

11. For an introduction to this discipline, see the journal, *Early Childhood Connections*, P.O. Box 4274, Greensboro, NC 27404-4274.

2. What Do the Numbers Tell Us?

1. This concept of the "awkward size congregation" is described in Lyle E. Schaller, *The Middle-Sized Church* (Nashville: Abingdon Press, 1985), pp. 99-137 and Lyle E. Schaller, *Looking in the Mirror* (Nashville: Abingdon Press, 1984), pp. 24-26.

3. What Is Our Purpose? What is Our Community Image?

1. An excellent introduction to this specialized ministry is Michael J. McManus, *Marriage Savers* (Grand Rapids, Mich.: Zondervan Publishing House, 1995).

4. Who Will Be Tomorrow's New Members?

1. If the goal is to move toward becoming a high-commitment congregation, two useful books on small groups are William J. McKay, *Nuts and Bolts Issues for Small Group Leaders* and David A. Paap, *Biblical Equipping*. Both are published by the Stephens Ministries in St. Louis and were designed for training leaders in the ChristCare Series, an excellent system for small group ministry.

5. How Are We Organized?

1. For a description of the small church style of ministry, see Lyle E. Schaller, *The Small Membership Church* (Nashville: Abingdon Press, 1994), pp. 11-40.
2. For a description of the large church style of ministry, see Lyle E. Schaller, *The Senior Pastor* (Nashville: Abingdon Press, 1988), pp. 21-122.

6. Means-to-an-End-Questions

1. This issue of trust is the central theme of Lyle E. Schaller, *Tattered Trust: Is There Hope for Your Denomination?* (Nashville: Abingdon Press, 1996), pp. 43-61.
2. The multisite option is discussed in Lyle E. Schaller, *Innovations in Ministry* (Nashville: Abingdon Press, 1994), pp. 112-33.
3. Ibid., pp. 64-111.

4. For a more detailed description of "Miracle Sunday," see Lyle E. Schaller, *44 Ways to Expand the Financial Base of Your Congregation* (Nashville: Abingdon Press, 1989), pp. 49-66.

7. How Large Should We Build It?

1. A superb introduction for public discourse in contemporary America is Kathleen Hall Jamison, *Eloquence in an Electronic Age* (New York: Oxford University Press, 1988).

2. For a longer discussion of the differences between the European religious heritage and the "Made in America" design of an institutional expression of the Christian faith, see Lyle E. Schaller, *The Interventionist* (Nashville: Abingdon Press, 1997), chapter 7.

3. Taken from Lyle E. Schaller, *Hey, That's Our Church!* (Nashville: Abingdon Press, 1975), p. 105.

4. For 190 other questions for your building planning committee, see Lyle E. Schaller, *Designing for Growth* (Cleveland: United Church Board of Homeland Ministries, 1993).

5. For alternatives in staffing smaller congregations see Lyle E. Schaller, *The Small Membership Church* (Nashville: Abingdon Press, 1994), pp. 124-27.

8. Three Fork-in-the-Road Questions

1. For a provocative review of the return on the investment in university-related divinity schools, see Conrad Cherry, *Hurrying Toward Zion* (Bloomington, Ind.: Indiana University Press, 1995) and W. Clark Gilpin, "The Theological Schools: Transmission, Transfor-mation, and Transcendence of Denominational Culture" in Jackson W. Carroll and Wade Clark Roof, eds. *Beyond Establishment* (Louisville: Westminster/John Knox, 1993), pp. 188-204.

2. Peter M. Senge, *The Fifth Discipline* (New York: Currency Doubleday, 1990).

3. Lyle E. Schaller, *Strategies for Change* (Nashville: Abingdon Press, 1993), pp. 67-78, 80-89, 110-12.

4. A. Paul Hare, *Handbook of Small Group Research*, 2nd ed. (New York: The Free Press, 1976).

5. The group of fived to three dozen individuals often is described as a social network. For an analysis of the power of social networks in evangelism, see Rodney Stark, *The Rise of Christianity* (Princeton: Princeton University Press, 1996) pp. 73-94.

6. A more detailed discussion of large group dynamics can be found in Lyle E. Schaller, *Effective Church Planning* (Nashville: Abingdon Press, 1979), pp. 17-63.

LINCOLN CHRISTIAN COLLEGE AND SEMINARY

254
SCH298F

93371

LINCOLN CHRISTIAN COLLEGE AND SEMINARY

3 4711 00094 9299